Texas
36th Division

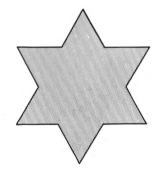

Sight Seein' Sixth
6th Division

Yankee
26th Division

Red Arrow
32nd Division

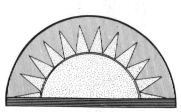

Jungleers
41st Division

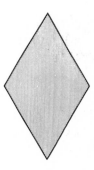

Red Diamond
5th Division

Sunshine
40th Division

Cross of Lorraine
79th Division

Rainbow
42nd Division

THE YANKS ARE COMING
The Story of General John J. Pershing

THE YANKS ARE COMING

THE STORY OF
General John J. Pershing

BY THE EDITORS OF THE
ARMY TIMES

1960

G. P. PUTNAM'S SONS · NEW YORK

To the A.E.F.

Published on the same day in the Dominion of Canada by Longmans, Green & Company, Toronto.

Library of Congress Catalog Card Number: 60-13667

MANUFACTURED IN THE UNITED STATES OF AMERICA

Contents

Foreword

For the second time in less than thirty years our troops celebrated with their Allies a victory in Europe.

On May 8, 1946, as "commander of this second American Expeditionary Force," General Dwight D. Eisenhower wrote to General Pershing:

> *I should like to acknowledge to you, leader of the first, our obligation for the part you have played in the present victory.*

And "Ike" amplified that part:

> *In the Mediterranean campaign of '42–'43 and the European operation of '44 and '45 a very important factor in American success has been the tactical judgment and skill and the identical command and staff conceptions of our regimental, division, corps and army commanders. These abilities and common doctrines have facilitated smoothness and speed in handling large formations and permitted a crushing application of tactical power. They have resulted directly from our magnificent military educational system, a system that was completely reorganized and expanded under your wise leadership and with your unstinting support.*

Newton D. Baker, President Wilson's Secretary of War, said of Pershing that he was puzzled how a man who thought so much about buttons could have such vision. Colonel Frederick Palmer, former news-paper correspondent and A.E.F. press censor, said of his long-time friend, the General of the Armies, "He was not given to phrases or promises. He was wholly aloof to any personal build-up. . . ."

He was surely "aloof," he was surely a man of "vision." Like George Washington, like Grant or Sherman, John Joseph Pershing appeared at a time of dire national peril.

In this centennial year, 1960, of General Pershing's birth, many Americans have realized it is time to reassess not only his contribution to history but to what we call our present way of life.

With not many words, but quite a few photographs, it is the hope of the editors that some approximation of the true measure of the man will be presented.

THE YANKS ARE COMING
The Story of General John J. Pershing

1

"Shoot Him, Pa!"

SEPTEMBER 13, 1860, came on a Thursday.

As on all other days that fall, the talk throughout the United States was of secession—and of the Presidential election. On the horizon there loomed unrelieved strife and dissension. None, certainly not Candidate Douglas or Candidate Lincoln, professed to see certain end in sight.

Internationally, although the Crimean War had been over four years, clouds were equally dark and threatening. There was fighting in China, wracked by interminable civil warfare. Damascus was seething following the execution of a Moslem, and the Turkish quarter had been sealed off.

Britain's warships were standing off half a dozen "trouble spots" in the East and Middle East.

Into such a world that Thursday, in Missouri, was born the son of a railroad section boss. It was a routine "frontier delivery," at tiny Laclede in Linn County. A couple of the neighbors' wives arrived at the frame shanty of John Fletcher Pershing and eased his wife, Ann, through her final labor pains.

John Joseph Pershing became the first child of this family of Alsatian descent, originally answering to the name "Pfirsching."

Like their ancestors, the Pershings of Laclede were industrious, direct-thinking, God-fearing folk. Ann Pershing, a bulwark of the Methodist Church, read the Bible to John—as well as to her subsequent surviving children—as some mothers might read Aesop, Hansel and Gretel, and the full lore of the nursery. The little boy's first heroes were those of the Old Testament: Joshua, Samuel, David and all the warriors before the time of Christ.

Warriors, in fact, dominated John's infant years. Before even his first birthday, the nation was engulfed in civil strife. The senior Pershing, sutler to the Eighteenth Missouri Volunteer Infantry, set up shop in the former general store in Laclede and moved his family in from the outskirts to a better one-story dwelling in the town. He also assumed the job of postmaster.

When the Eighteenth moved out, Pershing became sutler to another Missouri regiment mobilizing in Laclede. By 1864, his son was old enough to be aware of the men in blue uniforms swarming past his front yard, and of the peril which existed always, but a few hours, a few miles distant.

His "earliest recollection" was of a band of 30 southern "bushwhackers" under a desperado named Holtzclaw riding into Laclede, firing shots and then looting the place.

"Father," Pershing later recalled, "was postmaster and his store had grown to be the largest in town. Our residence was in the same block, five doors away, both the store and house being located on the north side of the public square. Here, just across the street and directly in front of the house, all male citizens who could be located were being rounded up by Holtzclaw's men. Some members of the band entered the store and father quietly left by the back way and went home. A couple of the raiders had just been to the front door of our house and demanded that father come out.

"Mother told them he was not at home and that if they did not believe her they might make a search. They had hardly left when father entered at the back. He brought with him his double-barrelled shotgun and went at once to the front window with the intention of firing on the raiders in the square; but mother, instantly grasping the situation, threw her arms around his neck and begged him not to be so rash."

Two citizens had already been shot for resisting. Holtzclaw finally herded the townspeople into the town square, harangued them for supposed Abolitionist sentiment and said the raid was in retaliation for "outrages committed upon his friends" to the south. They left as a Federal detachment neared Laclede.

A Home Guards company was formed after this, in which the senior

Pershing was a first lieutenant. Breastworks were erected on the outskirts of the town, which John and the other children of Laclede used as handy playgrounds.

By April, 1865, Mr. Pershing was one of the wealthiest citizens of Laclede and re-relocated his family in the two-story, gabled De Graw house, the most handsome residence in the community. At the same time, he purchased the village lumberyard and two large farms, as businesses in addition to his storekeeping and postmastership.

As the war ended, John started school—a private one operated by Miss Ella Seward, whose tuition fee was a modest 35 cents a week. She found the Pershing boy an "upstanding little youngster" with bright blue eyes and curling hair so light in hue that playmates teased him with the cry "Towhead!"

One week, Miss Seward noted in her diary that "Johnny" Pershing was "real sick with chicken pox and his eyes were affected." She called at his house, nonetheless, to read him his lessons.

Shortly, he went on to public school, where his first teacher was Miss Sally Crowder, whose father, David Crowder, had been killed in the Holtzclaw raid upon Laclede. There he proved a normal pupil, mastering his three R's and indulging in boyish pranks that caused the sterner disciplinarian of his teachers, "Old Man Angell," to switch his legs.

One time, at home, he found an old revolver and, while investigating its intricacies, sent a bullet crashing through his bedstead. This dangerous act brought down considerable parental wrath.

Discipline, however, was but one phase of the Pershing existence. The children led a balanced, happy life. John, for example, learned to ride horseback from his mother, "a superb horsewoman," whose favorite was a white-legged mount named Selim.

"Johnny's" boyhood contained ingredients, however, besides horseback riding, the old swimming hole and games of cops and robbers. The post-Civil War years were lawless ones, and the children of Missouri grew up all too aware of the names of Jesse James and the Younger brothers, whose example inspired many young men to become horse thieves.

"For some years," Pershing recalled, "the town was known as 'wild and woolly.' It was not uncommon during the six or seven years following the war for rough characters to come to town on Saturdays, carouse at the two saloons, and then gallop through the streets yelling and firing their pistols in the traditional manner of the Wild West."

The Pershing household was in marked contrast:

"My parents were God-fearing people and no Sunday passed that did not find the family attending either Sunday School or church and occasionally both. The Saturday night or Sunday morning tub was always a prerequisite to preparation for that day, when bright and early we were all turned out in our best clothes. Sunday was observed by most people in almost Puritan fashion, no games of any sort being permitted. Such rules were of course irksome to boys and girls and were often broken, but our parents were inclined to be liberal."

His father, for example, took the lead in obtaining funds for building a new Methodist church.

Young John read a variety of classics in his library at home, from Shakespeare to Poe, and the popular boys' books including *Robinson Crusoe* and the adventures of Daniel Boone and Davy Crockett. Beadle's "dime novels" were also something to be read, but surreptitiously. George Washington was his greatest hero.

The depression of 1873 hit the Pershings a blow that sent the head of the family reeling financially. Only 13, John had to learn farming, and learn fast. He did.

Among other bucolic accomplishments, the youth gained local fame by his ability to husk two rows of corn as fast as the average worker could go down one. As a Negro boy, Allen Warfield, who did some work for the Pershings, observed, "Johnny Pershing was a great cawn-husker, suh," also "a great hand to milk the cows and slop the hawgs."

Johnny's father tried to remedy his bankruptcy by leasing a small hotel, misappropriately named Palace, in Laclede. There seemed to be an eloquent scarcity of guests—and, when they did register, of paying guests.

Three years later he "hit the road" as a traveling salesman for a clothing store in St. Joseph at a salary of $2,000 a year. Finally, it seemed as though the family coffers would be replenished.

Possibly from sheer need to earn money, the junior Pershing turned to teaching, first—when he was but 17 years old, at a Negro school in Laclede. He had scant learning himself at that time, many of his 40 pupils were towering hulks and unruly, but—even as one of his oversized tormentors later observed—"He got that school in order, he had a quiet way but he meant business."

The pupil added, "One day I didn't know mah lesson, and he said, 'Moss, you stay in.' And he gave me a licking. Yas sah, it was a good licking, with a switch. . . . I knew mah lessons after that."

Pershing himself summed up his philosophy toward bullies or reluctant pupils: "My determination to deal with them directly and forcefully" would invariably bring "an end to the trouble."

In 1879, for the munificent salary of $35 a month, Pershing commenced teaching at the Prairie Mound district school, about 10 miles south of Laclede. There he was confronted with an awesome assortment of children and young adults, ranging in age from 6 to 21.

His first challenge came in the person of an overgrown, unruly teenage girl. Disciplining her, the new schoolmaster told her to remain in the classroom during lunch period. Instead, she scrambled through a window and ran home.

The next day she was at her desk as though nothing had happened. Again Pershing ordered her to remain in the room during lunch recess— and stayed himself to make sure. However, the defiant girl had slipped a note to her little sister, who herself hurried home.

Shortly, the children in the schoolyard saw a horse galloping posthaste down the road, leaving a trail of boiling dust in its wake. On it, leaning across the horse's neck and spurring the steed onward, was a man with red whiskers—and a shotgun. It was the girl's father.

The children stopped their play. They screamed and ran for cover beneath a nearby stone bridge.

Pershing, hearing their cries, looked out of the window. He needed only to look once to understand. He grabbed a poker from beside the potbellied stove and then walked deliberately to the steps of the schoolhouse.

"Let her out!" commanded the girl's father, now dismounted, and taking a bead on the schoolmaster's head.

"Shoot him!" screamed the girl, still in the room. "Shoot him, Pa!"

Pershing clutched his poker more firmly and walked toward the man who was threatening him.

"You may shoot me, sir," he said flatly, "but that is the only way you will obtain your girl's release until the end of classes."

"Shoot him, Pa!" his daughter repeated.

But "Pa" didn't shoot. And the girl wasn't "let out."

There was no more rebellion in the school at Prairie Mound, as young Pershing learned about teaching—and people.

West Point Cadet John Joseph Pershing. NATIONAL ARCHIVES

2

Second Lieutenant Pershing

"Johnny" Pershing may have satisfied himself that he had obtained mastery over the conduct of his pupils. But he was far less certain of his own "book learning."

This need that he had recognized in himself led him to enroll in the State Normal School at Kirksville, Missouri. In between terms, he continued to teach at Prairie Mound and even, in season, help with the crops on the family farm.

It was a horseback ride of several hours between Prairie Mound and Laclede. To Pershing, however, this was relaxation, pure enjoyment. A horse, once he was astride the animal, seemed almost a part of him, joined by sinews and nerve fibers.

As though his days were not sufficiently filled, John managed to squeeze in a little reading of Blackstone. He had an idea that when and if he tired of teaching he would become a lawyer, although he still believed that the former profession offered "the best chances available as a source of revenue."

He was deep in his lessons at Kirksville during the fall of 1881 when he noticed an item in the newspaper. It concerned a competitive examination for appointment to the Military Academy at West Point. He had never consciously thought of such a career before, but this seemed an opportunity to complete and perfect the education he so cherished.

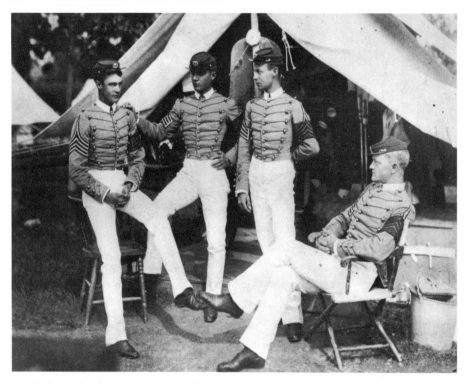

Young Pershing (*extreme right*) **graduated 30th in the Class of '86,
U. S. Military Academy.** PERSHING COLLECTION

He took the test and won his appointment over 16 others. His
mother, to his surprise, was dismayed at the news.

"But John, you are not going to be a soldier, are you?" she said in
anxiety.

But John most certainly was.

Commencing in January, 1882, candidate Pershing tutored at a preparatory school at Highland Falls, New York, directed by Colonel Caleb
Huse, former Confederate officer.

In June, he became one of 104 to enter the Academy.

His cadet days proved unspectacular. His marks were fair, he indulged in some Academy pranks, such as leaving his lights lit beyond 10
o'clock closing time, but never was involved in serious trouble. This was
expected since his best marks were in military discipline, his worst in
English.

Major General Wesley Merritt, a Civil War cavalryman, was super-
intendent of the Point at that time.

"Included among General Merritt's friends," Pershing recalled, "were Grant, Sherman, Sheridan and other great soldiers of the Civil War, several of whom came to visit West Point during my cadet days. I remember especially the stately figure of General Sherman as he took his daily walk about the post and how we used to consider it an especial honor to salute him."

In further recollections of undergraduate days, Pershing wrote:

"No one can ever forget his first guard tour with all its preparation and perspiration. I got along all right during the day, but at night on the color line my troubles began. Of course, I was scared beyond the point of properly applying any of my orders. A few minutes after taps, ghosts of all sorts began to appear from all directions. I selected a particularly bold one and challenged according to orders, 'Halt! who comes there?'

"At that the ghost stood still in his tracks. I then said, 'Halt! who stands there?' whereupon the ghost, who was carrying a chair, sat down, when I promptly said, 'Halt, who sits there?'"

Prom "trotters" to West Point during Pershing's undergraduate days. The girls, whose photograph is in the General's papers, are not identified. PERSHING COLLECTION

He was very proud of his class, as he added:

"The career of '86 at West Point was in many respects remarkable. There were no cliques, no dissensions; and personal prejudices or selfishness, if any existed, never came to the surface. From the very day we entered, the class as a unit has always stood for the very best traditions of West Point. The spirit of old West Point existed to a higher degree in the Class of '86 than in any class since the war."

Here he was nicknamed "Black Jack"—for no apparent especial reason—and here he rose to the presidency of his class and senior captain of Cadets. Soldiering had become as natural to him as horseback riding.

His roommate, Charles Walcutt, wrote:

"He was the leader of our class, not in his studies, but in everything else. He was conscientious, took the requirements of the Academy very seriously and gave his best in every element going to make up the sum total of life at that institution. He was a strict disciplinarian and one who observed very closely his own precepts.

"Some of his failures in recitation—and they came along as with most cadets—were painful, both to himself and to his fellow section mates;

Second Lieutenant J. J. Pershing went to active duty in the U. S. Army in the 80's in time to witness vestiges of Indian fighting such as pictured in this rare photograph. U. S. ARMY PHOTOGRAPH

one in English was heartrending, when he was required to discuss the subject of 'pseudo-metaphors,' while in the English course in the Fourth Class year. The subject was treated in the book in an abstract and technical way and was not clearly understood by any member of the section. Pershing was in no hurry to recite, but when called upon made a great struggle to clarify the subject. It was evident he had not made even a beginning in understanding it; however, he struggled on, greatly embarrassed, almost hopeless—great beads of perspiration standing out on his forehead. The instructor showed no disposition to throw any light or suggestion that might help. Instead that dignitary finally said: 'Mr. Pershing, what is a pseudo-metaphor?' That was the final straw that produced the collapse."

Of graduation day, Pershing, who ranked 30th in his class, recalled:

"As we took our places in ranks for the last time a very annoying lump arose in my throat. I had not realized that I was going to feel so deeply sentimental about it. I listened to the speech by General Sherman before he delivered our diplomas without remembering much that he said.

"Gratified, of course I was, to have reached the end of the four years, but loath to leave cadet days behind. They had been so fascinating, so gripping. It took a very positive exercise of the will to shake off the spell. . . ."

Members of the Class of '86 left West Point by steamer on June 14 for New York City and a celebration dinner at Martinelli's Restaurant. "Furlough Supper" the occasion was called.

Wrote the now Second Lieutenant Pershing:

"We finally reached the place finding the boys having a jolly time. A sumptuous supper was served, no loud or boisterous conduct occurred. Speeches were made by different members of the class, as the 'spirit' (s) moved them."

He reported that afterwards "the boys scattered about town for awhile but an early hour found them all in bed at their respective hotels."

The next day, Sunday, Pershing went sightseeing, impressed with the "beautiful buildings" of lower Broadway, including the Equitable Life and Tribune Building. The high spot was a walk across "the bridge," which was of course the Brooklyn Bridge, a marvel of the world. The young Army officers admitted they felt "quite shaky" traversing its long expanse. He felt constrained to list numerous facts and figures about the bridge in his diary.

He was an imposing officer. His classmates were proud of him. Some even professed to recognize in young Pershing the seeds of greatness. Robert Lee Bullard, one class ahead of him, wrote:

"Of regular but not handsome features and of robust, strong body, broad shouldered and well developed; almost or quite six feet tall; plainly of the estate of man while most of those about him were still boys; with keen searching gray eyes and intent look, Pershing inspired confidence but not affection. Personal magnetism seemed lacking. He won followers and admirers, but not personal worshippers. Plain in word, sane and direct in action, he applied himself to all duty and all work with a manifest purpose, not only of succeeding in what he attempted, but of surpassing, guiding, and directing his fellows in what was before them. His exercise of authority, was then and always has been since, of a nature peculiarly impersonal, dispassionate, hard and firm. This quality did not in him, as in many, give offense; the man was too impersonal, too given over to pure business and duty. His manner carried to the minds of those under him the suggestion, nay, the conviction, of unquestioned right to obedience. There was no shadow of doubt about it."

In September, Second Lieutenant Pershing commenced active duty with the Sixth Cavalry at Fort Bayard, New Mexico. The garrison at this lonely outpost had been engaged in stamping out the last resistance of hostile Indians led by the wily Geronimo.

In these badlands, once scourged by the Apaches, Chiricahuas and other warring tribes, Pershing still had ample opportunity to study both offensive and defensive guerrilla fighting.

One morning, word was flashed to the fort that three white men, surprised in their theft of a herd of cattle from some Zuni Indians, had killed three of the Zunis.

"The men," reported Pershing, "had retreated to a log ranch house where they were being besieged by the Indians. General Carr sent me to the scene with 10 men of my troop to investigate and do what was necessary. I found the Indians, 100 or more, greatly excited and determined to take the thieves dead or alive.

"They had completely surrounded the house and from a distance were keeping up a fusillade against it. It was not easy to persuade them to let me arrest the men, nor, after doing this, was it easy to induce these thoroughly scared prisoners to give up their arms.

"I had to go into the cabin, which they had barricaded, and personally demand it before they submitted to unconditional surrender. I

Pershing with the 6th Cavalry at Fort Bayard, New Mexico. He's sitting on the porch, legs crossed, holding the little girl. NATIONAL ARCHIVES AND U. S. ARMY

Lieutenant Pershing (*at left*) with U. S. Indian Commissioners, Indian scouts and other Army officers at Pine Ridge, South Dakota, 1891. U. S. ARMY

then put them on a buckboard and placing my troopers advantageously on either side rode back through the lines of threatening Indians and on to the post, where the culprits were confined in the guard house."

Shortly after this incident, the second lieutenant from Laclede, Missouri, distinguished himself by marching his men, complete with pack train, 146 miles in 46 hours over the roughest country.

Once, while encamped near Fort Niobrara, Nebraska, Pershing and his cavalrymen were all but submerged in a sudden plains blizzard. Although there had been no indication during the previous afternoon of the exceptional violence of the approaching storm, Lieutenant Pershing nonetheless had given orders to double-peg the tents—a precaution which doubtless saved many lives.

"I remember him," recalled Sergeant Tom Stevenson, "coming, all muffled up, to my tent just before the blizzard broke. He was always busy looking after the men, that's the sort of an officer Pershing was. And that's why the men would do anything for him."

One with exceptional affection for Pershing was an elderly Sioux Indian who had joined the Sixth Cavalry as a Scout. The Indian, drawing slowly upon his pipe, would sit outside the flaps of Pershing's tent all night, as his commander slept.

"Every time I moved," the lieutenant laughingly observed to a fellow officer, "that old Indian was on my trail."

The name of Lieutenant Pershing had become surprisingly familiar in the western part of the country—surprising considering his youth. The University of Nebraska, with a charter which provided for compulsory military training, was looking for a professor of military science and tactics. The faculty decided that they wanted the dashing officer from the Sixth Cavalry, and no one else.

In 1891, he became "Professor" Pershing, at Nebraska. The student publication *Hesperian*, in the months to come, offered testimony on this man of many talents, many emotions:

> *Pershing was as severe a disciplinarian as a kindly man can be. He was always just. He had no pets. Punishments for derelictions of duty came no swifter than his rewards for faithful performance.*
>
> *Lieutenant Pershing had a very keen, though grim sense of humor. How he laughed when we appeared for the first time in white duck trousers as part of our uniform. They were made under contract from measure by a concern which made tents and awnings, and the goods must have been cut out with a circular saw. . . .*

One day we had a grand review on the campus at which the Governor and other dignitaries were present. The Varsity Rifles battalion passed in review at quick time. The band had countermarched and played for us, and all went well. The second time around, however, was to be in double time. Lieutenant Pershing had given the band definite instructions, and the band-leader had solemnly assured him that they played double time as well as quick time. Pershing allowed that that was not saying much, but told him to go ahead anyhow.

When the band struck up its alleged double time, no thousand-legged worm could possibly have kept step with a single foot. The Battalion, which could drill in double time very well without music, immediately went to pieces and no route-step ever showed a greater variety of cadences.

Pershing stood it for a few minutes; then, realizing the hopelessness of the situation, broke into double time toward the band and yelled:

"Stop that band! Stop that awful band!"

The Governor, highly amused, shared Pershing's relief at the welcome silence.

John Pershing enjoyed four pleasant years at Nebraska, joining in the university dances with as much gusto as he did the drills and rifle practice. For, as Robert Lee Bullard had already observed at West Point, this lusty, vigorous Missourian was "a hop-goer, what cadets called a 'spoony' man. He loved the society of women."

Pershing didn't like schoolteaching. He had served his term at that as a civilian. The cadets thought he was taking out his gripe on them.

Irked by his iron discipline, a trick was perpetrated which the General did not forget.

It was Pershing's turn to inspect quarters and the cadets were prepared for vengeance. Cadets are supposed to wait in their quarters, officer's aide raps and immediately thrusts the door open, and the inspecting officer steps across the threshold.

The knock came. The door flew open and Pershing in dress uniform, which then included the beautifully plumed cavalry helmet, stepped in. Simultaneously a bucket of water hung just above the door poured down on him. The room was empty.

Later it developed the two occupants were elsewhere on special duty. No one would admit any knowledge of the affair. The entire barracks was put under discipline.

One very hot day Pershing called for an undershirt inspection.

The men took off their blouses and stood at attention while their shirts were inspected for presence, purity, and general pulchritude. The aide would call out the name of the cadet and the condition of his undershirt. Finally, he came to a South American. There was a pause while the aide caught his breath at what he beheld: "Cadet Garcia—*no shirt at all.*" Then the heavens fell.

3

Bullets and Wedding Bells

PERSHING, now a first lieutenant, was tactics instructor at West Point when the Spanish-American War broke out. Not until May, 1898, however, was he able to obtain orders back to his most recent outfit, the Tenth Cavalry.

By the end of June, Pershing, regimental quartermaster, was in Cuba, preparing along with the First Division of the Fifth Corps to storm San Juan Hill.

"The morning of July 1," he wrote, "was ideal, the sky cloudless, the air soft and balmy. Stately palms towered here and there above the jungle.

"Repose seemed to pervade nature. It was in no sense suggestive of war . . . from the ridge near the trail we could see the lines of the enemy's entrenchments and the blockhouses of the heights of San Juan. To the left of the hill, holding a horse, evidently that of his commanding officer, stood a lone Spanish orderly. Beyond could be seen the successive lines of defense, and the spires and towers of the city, El Caney, we were preparing to invest."

At 6:30 A.M. an artillery duel commenced, and about two hours later the Americans advanced up San Juan Hill.

". . . The road was narrow and torturous and was flanked by heavy jungle. Under the scorching sun, now high in the sky, it was like being in an oven. Our progress was slow and men began to drop out of ranks from

27

the heat. An occasional bullet nipped a leaf above our heads and our closed ranks began to suffer casualties. For some reason there was delay ahead of us and we halted for what seemed an hour."

The use of an Army observation balloon proved unfortunate. It followed the line of advance and thus brought Spanish fire upon the American forces. The attackers were relieved when the balloon descended.

About this time Pershing saw General William R. Shafter, the commanding officer; General Leonard Wood; and General Joseph "Little Joe" Wheeler, famed Confederate cavalryman, mounted again for this war. Pershing saluted Wheeler, and as he did so, ". . . a fragment of shell struck the water in front of him. He remarked very casually that the shelling seemed quite lively. Knowing that Sumner, the next in rank, was in command of the cavalry division that day I wondered why Wheeler was there. Later I learned that although on sick report he could not remain behind while his division was in action and simply had to come forward to be in the fight.

"When the hill was finally taken by storm the men cheered, shook hands with each other and threw their arms about each other and generally behaved wildly regardless of rank. American and Spanish soldiers lay dead around us and the wounded on both sides were cared for alike. A colored trooper stopped and gently raised the head of a wounded enemy lieutenant and gave him the last drop of water from his canteen. I assisted Lieutenant Short, Sixth Cavalry, in bandaging slight wounds."

Richard Harding Davis was also there, and he wrote his own vivid report:

". . . The thing which impressed one the most when our men started from cover was that they were so few. It seemed as if someone had made an awful and terrible mistake. One's instinct was to call to them to come back. . . .

"They had no glittering bayonets, they were not massed in regular array. There were a few men in advance, bunched together and creeping up a steep, sunny hill . . . the men held their guns pressed across their breasts and stepped heavily as they climbed. . . . They walked to greet death at every step, many of them as they advanced, sinking suddenly or pitching forward and disappearing in the high grass, but the others waded on, stubbornly, forming a thin blue line that kept creeping higher and higher up the hill. . . . It was as inevitable as the rising tide."

General Shafter, instead of being the rallying figure of the advance, was almost a travesty of a commanding officer—100 pounds overweight,

Lieutenant Pershing, along with the then much more famous Colonel Roosevelt (*above*), was at San Juan Hill, Cuba, in 1898. U. S. ARMY

The Rough Riders dig in after gaining San Juan Hill. U. S. ARMY

lame, short of breath, drenched in sweat. He confessed, pitifully, "I am prostrate in body and mind."

To young Pershing, Shafter's example "proved that officers must be in the best of health and vigor to stand the strain of war." Then he continued his diary:

"Early in the evening of the first day I accompanied the stretcher-bearers under charge of [Lieutenant Malvern Hill] Barnum carrying our Major T. J. Wint, who had been wounded, back to the field hospital at El Pozo. As we passed over the now quiet landscape its peaceful aspect under the brilliant moon presented a striking contrast to the day of battle just closed. En route we passed General Bates' brigade moving to take its place in our lines. The hospital presented another contrast. Many of the wounded had not yet received attention, as they had been brought in faster than the surgeons could care for them. The surgeons were now working under the dim lights of field lanterns."

The next day Lieutenant Barnum, classmate of Pershing's, was wounded. The latter assumed Barnum's post of regimental adjutant. During the day he came across Colonel Roosevelt and a detail of men trying to move their mired wagon: "He was urging his team forward with all the skill, including the forceful language of a born mule-skinner."

Pershing characteristically understated the events in his own diary, noting "I slept exceedingly well, better than I expected. I remember looking into the sky and wondering what the new day would bring forth. As I recall it now, all had a plenty of fighting. Capt. Kingsbury and I sat down and talked and smoked. He said he had enough."

On the morning of July 3, Shafter asked for surrender of Santiago. General Toral, refusing, nonetheless asked for a truce in which to evacuate civilians. The truce was granted, and the Americans then witnessed a strange and often sad sight.

"It was a dismal procession," wrote Pershing, "that streamed out of the city through our lines on the road to El Caney the following two days. Smart carriages drawn by well-groomed horses conveyed the consular officials, while primitive, creaking carts carried sick and infirm inhabitants and their poor belongings. The road was congested with vehicles, animals, and people on foot, old men and women hardly able to walk, young mothers with infants in arms, and toddling children, all laden with such of their belongings as they hoped to save."

On July 11, after desultory firing, General Toral surrendered.

There was display of bravery on both sides during the Cuban cam-

Strife was in Pershing's stars. The year after the war with Spain, he was in the Philippines, putting down the insurrection and pacifying the warring Moro tribesmen. This is a sample of the marshy terrain through which he led his troups. U. S. ARMY

Artillery, reminiscent of their Civil War counterparts, going into action against a jungle backdrop in the Philippines. U. S. ARMY

paign. The Spanish, ill-trained, ill-armed and overwhelmed numerically, fought with valor. The Americans, with better weapons but often with inadequate or lagging supplies, distinguished themselves for their own tenacity in a fever-breeding, steaming and unfamiliar terrain.

Pershing himself was singled out for praise by Lieutenant Colonel T. A. Baldwin, Tenth Cavalry commander and a Civil War veteran, as he told the young officer from Laclede:

"I have been in many fights and through the Civil War, but on my word you were the coolest man I ever saw under fire in my life, and carried out your orders to the letter no matter where it called."

The citation accompanying the Silver Star awarded Pershing for his conduct at San Juan Hill noted that Pershing "exhibited great bravery obeying orders with unflinching alacrity. . . ."

The end of the war found Pershing, along with many other veterans of the unhappy Cuban campaign, ailing. Malaria was the primary infection. When he left the hospital, he was ordered—much against his wishes—to a desk job in Washington. It involved administration of America's newly won possessions.

By the fall of 1899 he was en route to another conquered former Spanish possession: the Philippine Islands. There, assigned to the Eighth Army Corps, his mission was largely to help pacify, by any and all means necessary, the warring Moro tribesmen.

Each *dato*, or chieftain, presented his own challenge—mediation or frontal assault. The *dato* of the jungle fortress of Fort Bacolod, for example, scoffed at Lieutenant Pershing's warnings to lay down his arms.

"We will either live in peace or I must destroy you," asserted Pershing.

When the Moros attacked, Pershing made good his promise. He leveled the fortress of Bacolod as completely as some latter-day Carthage.

Yet, this was an exception rather than the rule of Pershing's methods in the Philippines. In fact, he won over most of the tribesmen to the extent where he was made an honorary *dato* himself. He wrote home of his popularity:

"The Sultan of Bayan asked me the other day to be an adopted father to his wife. I said I would. She is an Oato woman, and her father, dato Ami Ban Kurang, is very rich for a Moro. I have already three adopted children. One is the Raja-Muda of Oato. This means that he is heir to the Sultanate. Another is Tompogao, a bright, clean little fellow who has the airs of a Prince of Wales. He will be Sultan some day or a great dato. I have many very strong personal friends among the Moros. Some of them will do anything for me. If I should say, 'go and kill this man or that,' the next day they would appear in camp with his head."

His upperclassman friend from West Point, Lieutenant Bullard, serving with Pershing in the Philippines, wrote:

"The more I see of this unusual work the more I know that few men are fit to manage it, and the more I am of the opinion that General [George W.] Davis did right to keep Pershing in charge of these Moros instead of placing in charge some fool officer who ignorantly supposed that he could come and in an offhand manner manage these savages.

"In Pershing's services in the Moro country I also noticed his loyal adherence to the orders, plans, and wishes of his superiors. These were almost always contrary to the views and desires of brother officers and soldiers about him, and he was steadily and severely criticized for his strict adherence to those orders when he might have deviated from them; all of no avail—he still adhered. This then became or had already become —and has remained to this day—the marked characteristic of the man:

(*Left*) **A lean, stubborn fighter, Pershing leads his men to the attack on Fort Bacolod, Mindanao, April 8, 1903.** NATIONAL ARCHIVES

Pershing chatting with a local chieftain or "dato" in the Philippines. The chieftain, in white, is identified as "Pedro." NATIONAL ARCHIVES

loyal acceptance of and obedience to authority, no criticism or fault-finding with the plans and conduct of affairs by his superiors."

Pershing was rewarded with a promotion to captain. He had grown to like the Philippines so dearly that he requested continuance of orders.

As a captain, he was responsible for a relatively great number of officers and men. He won respect though, paradoxically, not close friendship. He commanded impartially, fairly, but with an iron fist.

One afternoon, he was seated in his tent in Mindanao when he heard a horse thundering by on the dirt jungle road. Rushing to the flaps, he shouted:

"Stop! Come here! Who are you?"

A lieutenant of the 19th Infantry dismounted and entered. He identified himself, matter-of-factly.

"Oh, that's different," said Pershing. "That changes the matter. I thought it was one of those ignorant cavalrymen of mine who don't know enough not to gallop a horse on a hard road!"

In 1903, Pershing was ordered back to the War Department. And that same year he met Helen Frances Warren, at a dinner party.

The daughter of Senator Francis E. Warren, of Wyoming, she had just graduated from Wellesley College. His reaction to her was electric.

"Charlie," he confided to a friend, Charles E. Magoon, "I've met the girl I'm going to marry."

The courtship was not quite the whirlwind as might have been forecast by Pershing's impetuous remark. A year, and duty in Oklahoma City with the Southwestern Division, was to intervene.

However, he visited the Warren ranch in Wyoming during the summer. In November, the Captain was back in Washington as a student at the Army War College. His wooing of Frances, a young lady her friends knew as "gay, warm-souled, of blithe originality," resumed.

On December 25, 1904, Pershing's diary proclaimed final victory:

"Spoke to F.E.W. and got his consent to marry Francis." (Captain Pershing invariably misspelled her name, unable to decide whether to use an "i" or an "e.")

However, approaching wedlock did not dazzle Pershing to the extent where he lost sight of the Army—or his abiding love of the cavalry. On December 30 he wrote his friend Malvern Hill Barnum, now a captain and recovered from his wounds in Cuba:

"You can rest assured that the cavalry officers of the General Staff and others here in Washington stand ready to do all they can to prevent

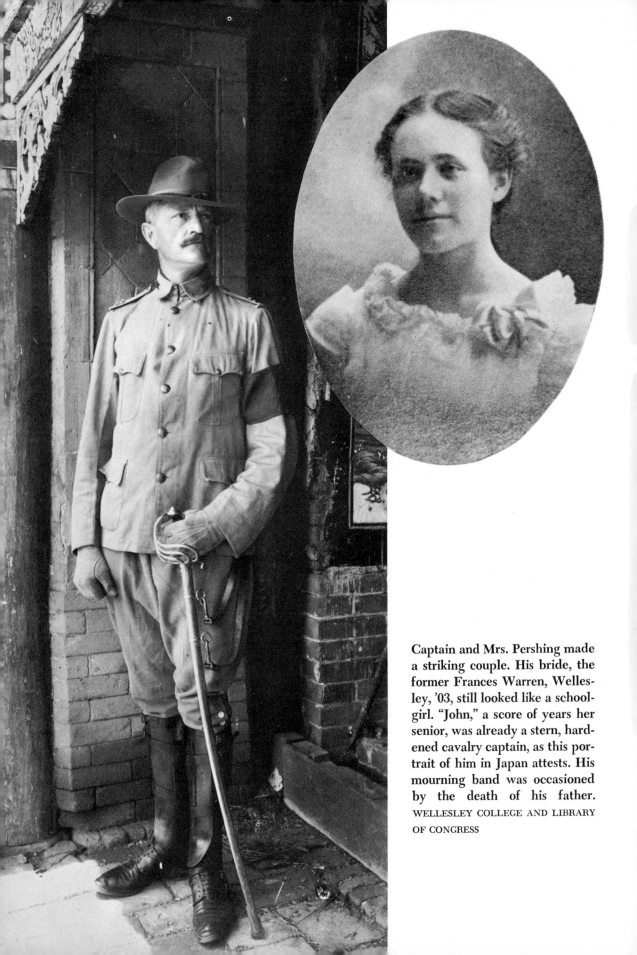

Captain and Mrs. Pershing made a striking couple. His bride, the former Frances Warren, Wellesley, '03, still looked like a schoolgirl. "John," a score of years her senior, was already a stern, hardened cavalry captain, as this portrait of him in Japan attests. His mourning band was occasioned by the death of his father.

the cavalry from being reduced, and also to retire a lot of old duffers at the top. . . . I think you can trust to the General Staff, not only the cavalry officers but all the others, to see that fair treatment is accorded all arms of the service in case of future Army legislation."

Early in 1905, Pershing's laconic diary entries continued to chronicle the change approaching in his life:

"January 11, 1905: Engagement announced in Washington *Post* and Frances and I danced the Bachelors German together. Were congratulated by everybody. She was divinely lovely that night.

"January 21: Ushers gave me a dinner—the best ever. Besides the ushers and best man, there were present Gen. Humphrey, Chauncey Baker McIntyre, Reber, Menoher, Dick Richardson, Jerry Taylor.

"January 26: Married at Church of the Epiphany at 12 o'clock. Reception and breakfast afterward at Willard Hotel. Ushers and best man and Francis' college friends, Alice Roosevelt, etc. . . ."

Captain Pershing did not confide to his diary, however, that Washington was struck by one of the severest blizzards in history that January 26. President Roosevelt, one of the guests and admirers of the groom, removed his overcoat and sprinted, chest out, through the blowing drifts of G Street and through the doors of the church.

Until February 15, the newlyweds had no honeymoon. They were too occupied with travel and official business until they quit San Francisco for Pershing's new station as military attaché in Tokyo. Again, this diary entry:

"Feb. 14: Sailed for Yokohama on Pacific Mail steamer *Korea*. Worst weather ever.

"Feb. 22 arrived in Honolulu. Frances seasick five days. Love her more and more. This is the dearest girl in the world and I the happiest man in the world."

4

Government Parsimony

CAPTAIN PERSHING and his bride landed in Yokohama and went on to Tokyo. He did not tarry there long since his orders called for him to be observer with General Kuroki's army in the Russo-Japanese war. He wrote:

"March 9: Completed preparations for leaving. Col. Wood turned over office and funds to me. Frances employed servants and we rented the house Woods live in. Finished packing and sent baggage down. Said goodbye to Frances. Saddest of all goodbyes. She is the dearest and bravest in the world. At the station she called 'Banzai, Jack!' "

Before he left he had made arrangements that his bride should receive some gift each day of his absence: flowers, candy, or some similar small remembrance.

He returned to Tokyo in September, and for the next year occupied himself largely with the routine of a military attaché. In September, 1906, two important events occurred in Pershing's life: the birth of his first child, Helen Elizabeth, and his commission as brigadier general by President Roosevelt.

It was a "jump promotion" over 862 officers senior to him, the vast majority of whom were beside themselves in anger. It was, as well, concluded one newspaper in perhaps an "inspired" editorial, a political promotion, since Pershing was Senator Warren's son-in-law. Roosevelt

Pershing in 1905 with Captain Tamaka when he was a U. S. Army observer in the Russo-Japanese War. NATIONAL ARCHIVES

himself was quick to defend his action, pointing out that Pershing had been promoted because of his work in the Philippines, prior to his marriage.

With his new position of responsibility, the 46-year-old general was ordered back to the Philippines, to command Fort McKinley.

For the next six years, the fortunes of the Pershing family were primarily interlinked with the Philippines. Though busy and, on occasions, fighting years they were nonetheless happy ones.

The family was increased by three more children: two girls and a boy. As commanding general of the Department of Mindanao and Governor of the Moro Province, he wrote of this phase of his existence:

"At Zamboango we led a life in the open air. The doors and windows of our house were always open in fair weather. When at home hardly a morning went by that we did not take a dip in the sea, which was but 20 paces away. When the tide was in we could dive off the end of our pier and when it was out we could wade to deep water over good sea sands. My wife was an excellent swimmer and the children took to the water like ducklings.

"But in this I was like an old hen. I was never at ease out of my depth and often fluttered about the shore in dismay when my wife would swim half a mile straight out into the sea.

"In the afternoon after 4 o'clock we often went horseback riding. Mrs. Pershing, having been raised on a ranch in Wyoming, was accustomed to horses. The children were taught as soon as they could sit on a pony, our son before he was three years old. . . .

"It was, I am sure, largely because of our active lives that we were able to remain in the tropics for such a long period. Though I was stationed at Zamboanga for four years we had no serious illness in the family except twice."

No man or officer of his command could boast greater strength, endurance or daring than J. J. Pershing. Within the jungled fastness of Mount Bagsak, hostile Moros had held out for some time. Finally, Pershing resolved to go in and get them by the employment of as much force as demanded.

First, the American Army removed the families of the warriors to places of safety. Even so, it was hoped until the last to avoid an open clash.

"Efforts," wrote Pershing, "did not cease until the outlaw conferees declared that they would never lay down their arms.

"The only principle for which they fought was the right to pillage and murder without molestation from the government.

"By this time the separation of the non-combatants from the desperadoes and criminals had been practically accomplished. Without further delay and without warning, the troops were called out.

"By a swift movement, Mount Bagsak was reached in the early morning of June 11th. The defenders of that mountain stronghold were caught unawares with most of their non-combatant followers absent and a very severe, though well-deserved, punishment was administered.

"Our course has met with the approval of the entire population of the Sulu archipelago. This Bagsak band of outlaws included some of the most notorious cattle-thieves and murderers that have ever infested the island. They had defied the officers of the law, fought the troops and opposed every attempt to establish order."

A master of understatement, especially where his own achievements were involved, the general did not mention that "he stood so close to the trench, directing operations, that his life was endangered by flying barongs and spears which were being continually hurled from the Moro stronghold." A junior officer supplied this eyewitness report.

Pershing, dismayed at what appeared to be brewing rewards for his valor, wrote to The Adjutant General in Washington:

1. I have recently been informed that a letter, supported by certificates and affadavits from officers and enlisted men, was sent some time ago to The Adjutant General of the Army, by Captain George C. Charlton, Philippine Scouts, recommending me for a Medal of Honor for distinguished gallantry in action against hostile Moros on Mount Bagsak, Island of Jolo, P. I., June 15, 1913.

2. While I highly appreciate the opinion of these officers and men, all of whom have served so faithfully, and who so gallantly performed their duties in this fight, I do not consider that my action on that occasion was such as to entitle me to be decorated with a Medal of Honor. I went to that part of the line because my presence there was necessary.

JOHN J. PERSHING

He followed this up with the half-gruff, half-joking admonition to Rowland Thomas, a magazine writer: "Don't you try to work in any hero stuff about me!"

Pershing's superiors were grateful nonetheless. He was awarded the Distinguished Service Medal for the Mount Bagsak expedition, and that he could not refuse.

The jungle fighter was now wearied, however. He welcomed approaching reassignment, in fact came back to the United States the long way around in order to travel by way of Europe.

"Service in the tropics," he wrote, "since the beginning of 1900 had not only run down my general health but had brought some anxiety as to the condition of my heart, and while abroad I visited Bad Nauheim, in Germany. The heart specialist there was not too encouraging and I returned to the States considerably alarmed. . . .

"I went on sick leave and became finally a patient at the Army and Navy Hospital in Hot Springs, Arkansas. Here I was given a thorough going-over by the staff under Colonel G. D. Deshon, a classmate of mine at West Point who had resigned to practice medicine and later had been appointed to the Medical Corps. The examination covered several days and, feeling apprehensive, I finally asked Deshon to tell me the worst.

" 'John,' he said, 'we have subjected you to every known test, and in my opinion and in that of my associates there isn't a damn thing the matter with you . . . tomorrow morning two saddle horses will be ready at 7 o'clock and we shall take a ride.'

"I was, I freely confess, in a blue funk. Convinced in my own mind that my heart would not stand the exertion and that the chances were less than even that I should return alive, I had to drive myself to appear the next morning, and still was skeptical when after a short ride no untoward results followed."

Still not entirely reassured, he settled down to duties as commandant of the Presidio, in San Francisco, and the Eighth Brigade.

Meanwhile, approaching strife was casting its ever-lengthening shadows across Europe. No one, however, realized the conflagration would come as soon or with such cataclysmic violence as actually was the case.

In 1914, the assassination in the Balkans of Archduke Francis Ferdinand, heir-apparent to the throne of Austria-Hungary, touched off a chain reaction of provocation, hysteria and stupid reasoning on the international level which culminated in the European war.

America watched in disbelief the distant eruption, at first not even taking steps to arm herself defensively.

"The fact is," wrote Pershing, as dismayed as any, "that the world knew only too well that we had for years neglected to make adequate preparations for defense, and Germany therefore dared to go considerably further than she would have gone if we had been even partially ready to support our demands by force."

General Pershing, however, was soon to be embroiled in troubles much closer to home—and this tinderbox was not kept smoldering by European, but Mexican, unrest. America's southern neighbor had experienced an unfortunate succession of inept or antagonistic presidents which, by 1914, had brought the two nations to the verge of conflict.

Sporadic civil war was ravaging Mexico. The inept president, Huerta, was opposed by General Carranza, who seized Vera Cruz, which was in turn occupied by United States forces. Huerta was forced to resign. Now Carranza's strongest opponent was Francisco "Pancho" Villa, who degenerated into unadorned banditry, killing peasant and government soldier with the same impartiality.

Obviously, whatever might happen internally an American army was needed to patrol the Mexican border. Major General "Scrapping Fred" Funston commanded the Army's largest unit, the Southern Department, headquartered at Fort Sam Houston, San Antonio. The leading general officer in the country, Funston had topped a distinguished career by singlehandedly capturing Aguinaldo, the Philippine insurgent.

The general wanted an able and resourceful second in command, and John Pershing appeared to be the unqualified answer to his needs. He brought the latter together with his Eighth Brigade from the Presidio and placed him in command of the Southwestern Division.

By the summer of 1915, war still had not erupted between the United States and its Latin neighbor. But it appeared that border clashes—at best an armed truce—would continue for the indefinite future. Pershing decided to move his family from the Presidio to El Paso and went about furnishing the quarters provided him at Fort Bliss.

Now, the Pershing family was growing up. His oldest daughter, Helen Elizabeth, was 8, Anne, 7, and Mary, 6. All were beautiful, curly-haired girls. His son, Francis Warren, was 5.

"I'm tired of living alone," he confided to another officer as he studied railroad timetables. His family's new home was ready.

Early on the morning of Friday, August 27, before the red dawn had quite blossomed over the hot Texas plains, Pershing was awakened by his orderly. Pale and obviously distraught, he held a telegram in his hand.

Its terrible message was told and retold in the nation's press. The San Francisco *Chronicle*, for one, reported:

> *Like the gallant wife of a gallant soldier, Mrs. Frances Warren Pershing, wife of Brigadier General John J. Pershing and a woman beloved throughout the Army, laid down her life yesterday morning at the Presidio in a vain effort to save her three little daughters from fire that demolished General Pershing's quarters.*
>
> *Mrs. Pershing was suffocated by the side of her children and when rescuers broke into her room through the smoke and flames, she was dead on the floor, her mother arms stretched protectingly over her little ones whom the fire also had claimed.*
>
> *General Pershing is today rushing here as fast as rail and steam can bring him from El Paso to claim the bodies of the wife and baby girls he loved better than all life, and to hold close to him the baby boy who, saved from the fire and uninjured, is the only surviving one of a little family that he said goodbye to at the Presidio only two weeks ago.*

There were twelve in the home, a two-story frame structure, at the time of the fire. Mrs. Pershing had been entertaining friends. She had retired, as customary, at 11 o'clock. Also, as customary, the coals in the dining room open hearth were left glowing.

About 4:20 A.M.—as the catastrophe was reconstructed—the coals spilled onto the highly waxed floor and instantly ignited. Thus, the General's family was victim to the Army's very fetish for "spit-and-polish," a fetish shared by the General himself.

Little Warren was saved by a Negro servant, Johnson, who managed to get the little boy out on a roof where firemen rescued him.

On Sunday, Pershing, his face like a granite mask, arrived in San Francisco and went directly to the Presidio. He stated: "I would like to see for myself just how it happened." When he emerged from the ruins he commented, "They had no chance."

In the afternoon, dressed in a frock coat and bowler hat, he attended funeral services at a San Francisco undertaker's, then left for Oakland and the burial in Wyoming.

The newspapers bitterly denounced "government parsimony" as responsible for the tragedy. Editorials pointed to the flimsy "shacks" that officers and other personnel of the important Presidio had to inhabit.

This stone at the Presidio, San Francisco, marks the site of the house where Frances Pershing and her three daughters perished in a nighttime fire. The plaque depicts what the quarters looked like in August, 1915, the month of the tragedy. U. S. ARMY

5

"... At as Early a Date as Practicable"

PERSHING spent a lonely, silent and withdrawn winter in the home at Fort Bliss that he had furnished for Frances, Helen Elizabeth, Anne and Mary. With him were only little Warren, his sister Miss Mae Pershing and—an orderly.

There were those who believed the General might lose his mind from grief. But they did not reckon with his soldier's discipline, the degree of self-control of which he was capable, his ability to submerge himself in his horseback riding.

The seeds of worsening U. S.-Mexican relations were flourishing like growing weeds under a June sun.

Villa, frustrated that the United States would not do the unthinkable—recognize his outlaw band as the legal government—hoped to foment war between his own country and its big northern neighbor. In January, he removed 16 Americans from a train and shot them.

When that failed to produce the internecine conflict he so passionately and insanely desired, Villa concocted a more drastic scheme to embarrass Carranza and embroil the two countries. Just before dawn, March 9, Thursday, with a band of 500, he galloped across the border and into Columbus, New Mexico.

Shouting "Viva Villa!" and "Death to Americans!" they surprised the 13th U. S. Cavalry stationed there.

Pershing in a rare, "happier"-days photo with Pancho Villa, on his right, whose outlaw band he was to pursue into Mexico. On Villa's right is General Huerta, one of a succession of inept Mexican presidents. PERSHING COLLECTION

Rather amazingly, since they had been caught unawares, the soldiers rallied to counterattack, then pursued Villa across the border. Eight Army men were killed and the same number of Columbus civilians. Villa lost more than a third of his brigands.

Generally slow to anger, President Wilson reacted quickly and decisively. He hurried an order to the War Department, which conveyed it to General Funston in San Antonio:

"An adequate force will be sent at once in pursuit of Villa, with the single object of capturing him and putting a stop to his forays!"

Remarkably enough, with Pershing as their leader, a hastily mobilized "punitive expedition"—nearly 10,000 strong—was in a few days churning up the dust of Mexico in pursuit of the bandit. On other scores, there was little to boast about, even as at Bull Run of yesterday.

The Quartermaster Corps proved all too readily that it possessed no emergency plans whatsoever. Freight cars banged into the Columbus railroad station, sealed and, in many instances, packed until they bulged —and yet none of them labeled as to contents. Trucks, dispatched posthaste from Army camps as far distant as Riley, in Kansas, rolled into Columbus—with no boxes of spare parts.

Worse yet, massive crates of brand-new trucks and other Army vehicles arrived at the border, supposedly ready for assembly. It turned out, when far too many of the crates were opened, that chassis and body were mismates—Model T Ford frames, for example, and Mack truck upper parts.

Heroically, the Flying Service of the Signal Corps dispatched eight airplanes to Columbus. Two were found in such deplorable condition that they were broken up and burned at once. A third crashed on its first foray over the border, although the pilot and observer were able to slog, parched with thirst and starving, over 65 miles of desert to the nearest Army outpost.

The surviving machines flew, after a fashion, as long as their devoted pilots and patient mechanics could keep them in the air.

At 56 years of age, Pershing set a hammering pace which exhausted many much younger cavalry officers. Here he is leading his men into Mexico, March, 1916. NATIONAL ARCHIVES

It was, patently, no way to fight a war, not even to prosecute a border "incident."

"Under the orders he received," wrote his friend Colonel Bullard, commanding another segment of the expedition, "he had as much chance to get Villa as to find a needle in a haystack. He must have known this before he started, yet nowhere does he seem to have broken over the restraining conditions of these orders. Down at Brownsville, when I heard of his selection and his orders, I said, 'He will obey his superiors absolutely. Had the President searched the whole Army over to find a commander of this expedition he could probably have found no other who would be ready so absolutely to obey his instructions and comply with his wishes in every respect.'"

Everything seemed against him. It was difficult to bring supplies in. Even the American railroads were threatening to strike. Because of Army red tape, it was equally impossible to procure food on the route of march. A Cusihuiriachic native, for example, described the problems as follows:

"You Americans pay for food all right, but you give receipts only. Now you buy a cow from a man who lives a hundred miles from any

The U. S. Army troops who pursued the bandit Villa found a sun-parched wasteland of desert, low hills and scrub growth. U. S. ARMY

The few trucks that rolled into Mexico were misassembled or otherwise incapable of top performance. For the most part, Pershing, like General Grant, depended on horses and wagons as his supply train.

railroad. Even if that railroad were operating it would be six months before he could get his mail. You take that cow and you kill it and you give him a receipt. He mails that receipt to the Quartermaster at San Antonio in Texas. It takes maybe six months for it to get there, if it gets there at all. When the Quartermaster gets it he cannot pay for it. He returns duplicate vouchers to be signed. They take another six months to reach the man, and then he cannot write and he cannot read English. If he can do all these things and signs in the proper place—even then he gets, about 18 months later, a check that he cannot cash."

On March 29, one column clashed with a rear guard of Villa's bandits. Another column, on April 12, pushed to Parral, more than 100 miles south of the New Mexican border, only to be surprised in the night and forced to retreat 15 miles.

Nonetheless, in the face of disheartening conditions and improper support, Pershing persisted. On June 16, he wrote from his field headquarters at Casas Grandes to General J. B. Trevino of President Carranza's federal forces:

One of Pershing's few scout planes lands on the Mexican border near a supply train. NATIONAL ARCHIVES

I am in receipt of your telegram advising me that your government had directed you to prevent any movement to the south, east or west of the American forces now in Mexico, and that should such movement take place the American forces will be attacked by Mexican forces. In reply you are informed that my government has placed no such restrictions upon the movements of American forces. I shall therefore use my own judgment as to when and in what direction I shall move my forces in pursuit of bandits or in seeking information regarding bandits. If under these circumstances the Mexican forces attack any of my columns the responsibility for the consequences will lie with the Mexican government.

Respectfully yours

Near Carrizal, five days later, a clash ensued in which 10 Americans were killed, 23 were taken prisoner. Neither side having covered itself with glory, the opponents settled down once more to eye one another like two cats which never really had wanted to fight in the first place.

"Trail-weary though they were, scorched by the blazing mid-day sun," he wrote in tribute of his men, "and chilled by the cold night breezes, subsisting on the country and frequently hungry in consequence, they never lost heart but day after day doggedly stuck to their task."

Pershing himself met praise from most quarters. Junius B. Wood, for example, correspondent for the Chicago *Daily News*, wrote:

General Pershing is a tireless worker. A light may burn in his tent until early morning, while he sits alone reading over reports and planning moves for future days. He may be up at daylight walking through the sleeping camp and observing with his own eyes. He believes in keeping men busy, officers and privates.

"Don't let them stagnate," he says. "Idleness has ruined more armies than battles have."

Wood added, "The General believes in asking questions. A group of reporters never approaches but he has as many questions as they have."

Unbeaten, arrogant and as lawless as ever, Villa by December was still threatening to "wipe out!" Pershing's expedition. However, it ap-

Brigadier General Pershing in a semi-candid pose while encamped in Mexico—emerging from the officers' breakfast tent. NATIONAL ARCHIVES

peared at last as though President Carranza and President Wilson were reaching accord. In effect, Carranza promised more effective measures to rid his country of bandits such as Villa if the U. S. Army would please go home.

In February, the tired, dusty soldiers—regulars and National Guard—did just what the Mexican president had implored.

Time, now, was almost used up on the international scale. Unrestricted submarine warfare had inflamed the passions of Americans like some modern-day Bunker Hill. They remembered Louvain, the *Lusitania*, the shooting of Edith Cavell, and a dozen provocations or, in some instances, fancied provocations. In their callowness regarding the world as it took up beyond Ambrose Channel and Daytona Beach, they felt that if they joined in the European war they could somehow make everything all right again.

Wilson had suggested to the belligerents in January a "peace without victory." But they did not want peace, even though war on the Western Front was a bloody, wasting stalemate. From the Kaiser's point of view it looked as though the Central Powers were going to win: their largest single adversary, Russia, was wracked with revolution, almost out of the fight.

The French, with the principal exceptions of Foch, Joffre and Pétain, were poorly led by general officers. The British Army was holding and, in areas such as Cambrai and Bapaume, even advancing; the B.E.F.'s staff work, however, left much to be desired, even as that of the French. The bungled Somme offensive was an obvious case in point.

The sands in the hourglass of American neutrality had now run out. On April 2, Woodrow Wilson went before Congress to assert:

" . . . the recent course of the Imperial Government . . . nothing less than war against the Government and people of the United States. . . . We are now about to accept gage of battle with this natural foe of liberty."

On April 6, 1917, America was in the war.

An American Expeditionary Force was needed—and a leader. Pershing, now a major general and commanding the Southern Department following General Funston's sudden death, was an obvious choice. And he would have been even if he were not the son-in-law of the influential Senator Warren.

Called to Washington, Pershing was ushered into the office of Secre-

Pershing reading in front of his tent flaps, in Mexico.

tary of War Newton D. Baker on May 10. Pershing's own diary recorded the momentous news:

"Occupied General George Davis' apartments at the Connecticut. Reported to the Secretary of War at about 10:30 A.M. Was informed by the Secretary that I was to command the American troops in Europe, and that I should be prepared to leave for France as soon as possible . . . remained at War Department until about 6:30 P.M."

Major General Pershing was not to be spoiled by the extravagance of time for preparation. A week later the War Department proclaimed the First Division in being, and the next day ordered the almost paper entity to prepare to sail for the battlefront.

On May 19, President Wilson himself instructed Pershing and the division "to proceed to France at as early a date as practicable."

The Chicago Daily Tribune.

FINAL EDITION

This Paper Consists of Two Sections—SECTION ONE

DO YOUR BIT NOW + JOIN THE RED CROSS

THE WORLD'S GREATEST NEWSPAPER

VOLUME LXXVI.—NO. 120. C. [COPYRIGHT: 1917, BY THE TRIBUNE COMPANY.] SATURDAY, MAY 19, 1917.—TWENTY-SIX PAGES. * * PRICE TWO CENTS.

PERSHING ARMY TO FRANCE

ALL JOIN HANDS IN SOLUTION OF FOOD PROBLEM

Allies to Liquidate Options —Grain Men Indorse Board of Control.

(By a Staff Correspondent.)

Washington, D. C., May 18.—[Special.]—Representatives of grain exchanges of the United States, officials of government departments, commissioners of the European allies, members of congress, and Herbert C. Hoover, prospective food controller of the nation, were busily engaged today in conference looking to the solution of domestic and international food problems occasioned by the war.

LIMIT GRAIN EXPORTS.

Among important developments of the day were the following:

Decision by the government to limit grain exports to the neutral nations, Sweden, Norway, Denmark, Switzerland, Holland, and Spain, a system of rationing to be devised absolutely under direction of a food control commission to be created by congress.

Agreement by the European allies to liquidate their enormous options on American grain futures, much of which could not be delivered, and to coöperate with the United States in a pooling system whereby exports will be apportioned with due regard to domestic requirements.

Formulation of plans for controlling the wheat output of the country agreed to by representatives of the grain exchanges in conference with Mr. Hoover, these to be submitted to the exchanges for approval pending action in congress on administration food control legislation.

Acquiescence by the special committee of grain exchanges for national defense in the government proposal for a food commission independent of any existing government department, the administration of such commission to be limited to the period of the war.

URGES MAXIMUM PRICES.

Recommendation to the house agricultural committee by Special Food Investigator George A. Anderson for legislation empowering the government to fix maximum prices for foodstuffs and to break up corners in foodstuffs by seizing and marketing products held by hoarders or unfair traders.

Charges of the existence of conspiracies in various sections of the country on the part of middlemen to boost prices turned over by the department of agriculture to the attorney general for investigation and probable prosecution.

Bills introduced in congress, one by Representative Webb of North Carolina, for prohibition of use of food products in the manufacture of liquor, and one by Representative Esticen of Illinois to prohibit slaughter of female cattle under 3 years of age and male cattle under 1 year, as a means of conserving the beef supply.

GRAIN MEN FOR FOOD BOARD.

One of the more gratifying developments to the administration has been the cordial relations established between the grain exchange men and Mr. Hoover in their informal conferences, which have brought to an end temporarily tonight.

At the end of the conference the grain men issued a formal statement indorsing the plan for establishment of a food board. Those who joined in the statement were C. B. Pierce, J. C. F. Merrill, J. Ralph Pickell, and Robert McDougal of Chicago; F. B. Wells and J. H. MacMillen, Minneapolis; George Aylesworth, Kansas City; N. L. Moffit, St. Louis, and Julius H. Barton, New York.

The grain men took back with them some recommendations relating to wheat options and transportation which they will submit to the various exchanges and will report back to Mr. Hoover after exchange has enacted the food laws now being considered by the committees on agriculture.

SHIPMENTS TO NEUTRALS.

While Mr. Hoover and the American grain experts were in consultation an important international food conference was being held at the state department.

The principal subject discussed was the problem of furnishing foodstuffs to the neutral nations of Europe, particularly to the Scandinavian countries, which have been under suspicion from time to time of transhipping supplies to Germany. Arthur J. Balfour, the British foreign secretary; Lord Eustace

(Continued on page 6, column 3.)

SOMEWHERE IN FORT SHERIDAN

[Copyright: 1917: By John T. McCutcheon.]

YOU MAY NOT ENVY THE ROOKIES JUST NOW, BUT—

JUST WAIT A FEW WEEKS AND YOU WILL.

THE WEATHER.

SATURDAY, MAY 19, 1917.

Sunrise, 4:57; sunset, 7:07. Moon rises at 2:41 a. m. Saturday.

Chicago and vicinity: Partly cloudy Saturday; not much change in temperature; moderate winds, becoming unsettled by Sunday; warmer Saturday; cooler Sunday; moderate to fresh winds.

Illinois—Generally fair Saturday; warmer in northeast portion; Sunday partly cloudy, cooler in north portion.

BAROMETER.

TEMPERATURE IN CHICAGO.

Maximum, 5 a. m. 73
Minimum, 8 p. m. 61

YESTERDAY ELSEWHERE.

CAMERONIA SUNK; 140 ARE MISSING FROM TRANSPORT

Hidden U-Boat Deals Death — Thrilling Rescues at Sea.

LONDON, May 17.—[Delayed by censor.]—It is announced officially that the transport Cameronia has been sunk. One hundred and forty men on board are missing.

The British admiralty statement follows:

"The British transport Cameronia with troops was torpedoed by an enemy submarine in the eastern Mediterranean on April 15. One hundred and forty men are missing and are presumed to have been drowned."

Many Killed by Torpedo.

The survivors of the Cameronia say the vessel was torpedoed in fine, calm weather in the afternoon. The submarine was not seen.

A large number of the casualties were due to the explosion of the torpedo, which struck where there happened to be many soldiers. There was some excitement and confusion at the moment after the torpedo had struck, but discipline soon prevailed. The boats were smartly launched, but one of them was smashed and many lives were lost.

Picked Up from Sea.

The Cameronia was afloat for about forty minutes after it was torpedoed, which enabled torpedo boat destroyers to run alongside the doomed vessel. Soldiers both in disciplined succession.

Several tales are told of gallant rescue. Chief Officer McMorris said while trying to save a drowning soldier. Max Burnie was a survivor of the Ancona liner disaster California when it was sunk off the Irish coast by a submarine on May 1, 1915.

David-W. Bone, commanding the Cameronia, was the last to leave the steamer. Rockwell and Forty-eighth streets, in jumping from the bridge to the wireless apparatus of a torpedo boat destroyer.

CRAFT OF 11,000 TONS.

The British steamer Cameronia (10,963 tons) was one of the largest ships belonging to the Anchor line of Glasgow. It was 515 feet long, 58 feet in width, and 317 in depth.

The Cameronia was launched at Glasgow May 27, 1911, and arrived in New York on its maiden trip across the Atlantic Sept. 21 of that year.

TWO DIE IN FIRE WHICH DESTROYS $250,000 PLANT

Two workmen were burned to death, six others had to jump through windows to escape a similar fate, and property valued at approximately $250,000 was destroyed late last night when an explosion of acetylene gas set fire to the plant of the Standard Spiral Pipe company. Forty-eighth streets, in the one story brick structure, covered an entire block.

Eight men were working in the building at the time. Tony Bellenic, a fireman, was one of the victims. The other was a laborer known only as "Mike."

German Women Give Hair for Belts in War Plants

COPENHAGEN, via London, May 19.—The Women's Patriotic league of Solingen, Rhenish Prussia, (Germany,) is making a collection of women's hair from which is woven belting for use in munition works. Shorter hair will be used to make felt for military purposes.

THE WAR

UNITED STATES.

President Wilson orders U. S. army to France. Gen. J. J. Pershing named to lead first division of 28,000 men.

President issues proclamation calling on all men subject to selective conscription to register June 5.

U. S. and entente officials, aided by American grain men, pave way for solution of food problem. Allies to liquidate options. Board of food control is formed.

Republicans in house block move to prevent certain duties in war fund asked.

ABROAD.

London reports British heavy artillery aiding Italians on Austrian front. Rome reports repulse of Austrian counter-attacks. Prisoners since opening of offensive total more than 6,000.

London officially reports sinking of liner Cameronia. One hundred and forty men on board missing.

Official report from Vienna says British cruiser was sunk in battle of Italy. London admits destruction of fourteen drifters, but denies loss of warship.

ORDERS OF PRESIDENT.

The president's proclamation, after quoting the essential sections of the new law (printed on page 2 of this paper), goes on to say:

"I, Woodrow Wilson, president of the United States, do call upon the governor of each of the several states and the territories, the board of commissioners of the District of Columbia, and all officers and agents of the several states and territories, of the District of Columbia, and of the counties and municipalities therein to perform certain duties in the execution of the foregoing law, which duties will be communicated to them directly in regulations of even date herewith.

"And I do further proclaim and give notice to all persons subject to registration in the several states and in the District of Columbia in accordance with the above law that the time and place of such registration shall be between 7 a. m. and 9 p. m. on the 5th day of June, 1917. At the registration place in the precinct wherein they have their permanent residence.

"Those who shall have attained their twenty-first birthday and who shall not have attained their thirty-first birthday on or before the day here named are required to register, excepting only officers and enlisted men of the regular army, the navy, the marine corps, and the national guard and naval militia in the service of the United States, and officers and enlisted men in the enlisted reserve corps while in active service.

REGISTER ON JUNE 5.

"In the territories of Alaska, Hawaii, and Porto Rico a day for registration will be named in a later proclamation.

HOW TO USE MAP.

"And I do charge upon every thoughtful citizen that the aim of this great conscription may be accomplished with as little bitterness and resentment as possible."

JUNE 5 MADE REGISTRY DAY FOR THE DRAFT

All Men Between 21 and 30 Inclusive Must Appear.

(By a Staff Correspondent.)

Washington, D. C., May 18.—[Special.]—President Wilson tonight issued the proclamation setting at work the machinery by which 10,000,000 men will be registered, creating the body from which eventually 2,000,000 American soldiers will be chosen by selective conscription.

All of these 2,000,000 will not be chosen at once, the first contingent being 500,000 men for the new army, with the possibility of conscription to fill the regular army and the federal militia to their authorized war strength.

The president's action was taken after he had signed the bill passed by congress granting him the authority to call on the young men of the nation to fill the requirements of universal selective service.

MEN WHO MUST REGISTER.

Under the proclamation issued tonight, every man who is in the prescribed age limits and who is not already in the service of the nation must register on Tuesday, June 5, by the division of regular soldiers for active service.

"The 'law under which registration is issued makes it plain that they who register must have attained their twenty-first birthday before June 5. Likewise, all those who 'have not attained their thirty-first birthday before June 5' must register.

"All persons so registered," the law adds, "shall be and remain subject to draft into the forces authorized, unless exempted or excused therefrom as in this act provided."

WILSON REJECTS ROOSEVELT U. S. VOLUNTEER SCHEME

WASHINGTON, D. C., May 18.—[Special.]—In declining to create the volunteer division for Col. Roosevelt's proposed President Wilson tonight made this statement:

"I shall not avail myself, at any rate at the present stage of the war, of the authorization conferred by the act to organize volunteer divisions. To do so would seriously interfere with the carrying out of the chief and most immediately important purpose contemplated by this legislation, the prompt creation and early use of an effective army, and would contribute practically nothing to the effective strength of the armies now engaged against Germany.

"I understand that the section of the act which authorizes the creation of volunteer divisions in addition to the draft was added with a view to providing an independent command and Mr. Roosevelt and giving the military authorities, an opportunity to use his fine vigor and enthusiasm in recruiting the forces now at the western front.

"It would be very agreeable to me to pay Mr. Roosevelt this compliment and the allies the compliment of sending to their aid one of our most distinguished public men, an ex-president who has rendered many conspicuous public services and proved his gallantry in many striking ways. Politically, too, it would no doubt have a very fine effect and make a profound impression. But this is not the time or the occasion for compliment or for any action not calculated to contribute to the immediate success of the war.

"The business now in hand is undramatic, practical, and of scientific definiteness and precision. I shall act with regard to it at every step and in every particular under expert and professional advice, from both sides of the water.

"That advice is that the men most needed are men of the ages contemplated in the draft provisions of the present bill, not men of the age and sort contemplated in the section which authorizes the formation of volunteer units, and that for the prompt and undisturbed use of the men who are to be drafted we shall need all of our present resources.

"Mr. Roosevelt told me, when I had

COLONEL IS SILENT.

Oyster Bay, N. Y., May 18.—[Special.]—What Col. Theodore Roosevelt's reply to President Wilson's refusal to give the offer of a Roosevelt volunteer army for service in France be learned directly to the refusal of the president's statement service has been mere sweet simplicity than a volunteer force.

"I have nothing to say tonight," he said finally. "I tried to President Wilson this afternoon offering to raise two divisions for immediate service and, if he so desired, two others.

"The first troops sent to France will

be taken from the present forces of the regular army and will be under the command of trained soldiers only.

"The responsibility for the successful conduct of our part in this great war rests upon me. I could not escape it if I would. I am too much interested in the cause we are fighting for to be interested in anything but success. The issues involved are too immense for me to take into consideration anything whatever except the best, most effective, most immediate means of military action.

"What these means are I know from the mouths of men who have seen war as it is now conducted, who have no illusions, and to whom the whole matter is a business of business. I shall render my selection upon these means and let everything else wait. I should be deeply to blame should I disappear, whatever the argument of politics or of personal gratification or advantage."

WILSON PICKS 28,000 MEN TO SAIL SOON

Cream of Regulars Makes Up First Contingent from the U. S.

BY ARTHUR SEARS HENNING.

Washington, D. C., May 18.—[Special.]—President Wilson tonight issued orders for the dispatch of the first expeditionary force to France.

This expedition, which will be sent to the firing line as soon as possible, will consist of one division of regular army troops—28,000 men—and will be under the command of Maj. Gen. J. J. Pershing, who led the American army in pursuit of Villa in Mexico last year.

Gen. Pershing to Command.

The announcement of the decision to place the American flag on the firing line at once was made in the following press bulletin issued by the war department:

"The president has directed an expeditionary force of approximately one division of regular army troops, under command of Maj. Gen. Pershing, to proceed to France as early a date as practicable. Gen. Pershing and staff will precede the troops abroad.

"It is requested that no details or speculations with regard to the mobilization of this command, dates of departure, composition, or other items be carried by the press, other than the official bulletins given out by the war department relating thereto.

Army of Picked Units

"The division sent to France will consist of picked units of the regular army. All the men will be veterans of the service. They will go into a camp near the front in France, where they will receive intensive training in the most approved methods of trench warfare under the direction of French and British officers.

"Although it is not permitted to discuss the plans for mobilization and departure, it may be taken granted by the American people that the American troops will be giving an account of themselves in the common cause with the French and British allies by the end of the summer operations.

Answer to Allies' Appeal

"The administration by announcing this decision to expedite the dispatch of troops has acquiesced in the behalf of the British and French war missions for American military aid in the present campaign on the western front.

"Gen. Joffre informed the president that even one division of American troops not only would lend great encouragement to the allied forces but would be of great actual assistance in the fighting.

"The difficulty of undertaking to transport a division and keep arms and supplies it will run has been solved in negotiation with the allies. A certain number of vessels not needed for transportation of food and munitions to the allies will be set aside as transports for the reactionary force.

(The exclusive cablegram)

PREMIER URGES CANADA TO OPEN DRAFT SERVICE

Ottawa, Ont., May 18.—Compulsory military service on a selective basis to raise immediately at least 50,000, and probably 100,000, men to keep the Canadian troops now in France up to proposed to parliament late today by Sir Robert Borden, the premier, who returned from England last Tuesday.

The prime minister declared that every man in the country had been given the opportunity, under the voluntary enlistment plan, to do his duty to the country and to the cause. Under this plan Canada had done well, he said. There had been dispatched 332,000 men to the Canadian forces across the seas.

But more are needed, Sir Robert announced. There were under cross examination to supply reinforcements to keep the five Canadian army divisions up to strength for some time. In the last five years wastage and provision had to be made for the future unless the five Canadian divisions were to dwindle to four, to three, and to two.

Mrs. John J. Mitchell's Son Accepted in Aviation Corps

William M. Mitchell, 21, oldest son of and Mrs. John J. Mitchell, 1500 North Dearborn parkway, has been accepted for the aviation corps. Mrs. Mitchell, who offered her three sons to the nation before war was declared, said last night that she was delighted that her wish had been fulfilled in part, at least.

Mr. Mitchell is president of the Illinois Trust and Savings bank. William M. is a graduate of Harvard, June 2. He has been attending Yale, and Charcoar is at the Middlesex school, Concord, Mass.

Another Chicagoan Falls While Fighting in France

Ottawa, Ont., May 18.—H. C. Douglas of Chicago was listed in today's official casualty report as wounded while fighting with the Canadian forces in France.

Pianos Due to Join Higher Cost of Living Parade?

LATE NEWS BULLETINS

• PARIS, May 19.—A resolution calling for the independence of Lithuania, in close union with France, England, Russia, and the United States, has been adopted at a meeting of 1,000 natives of the principality, under the presidency of Count Zamoyski. A copy of the resolution was presented to United States Ambassador Sharp for transmission to President Wilson.

• Boston, Mass., May 18.—The arrival in Switzerland of a party of American missionaries from Turkey, headed by William W. Peet, was announced today through cable dispatches received from Berne by the American board of commissioners for foreign missions. Another cablegram reported that a large number of teachers from Robert college and the Constantinople colleges for girls had reached Switzerland.

• Washington, D. C., May 18.—Pope Benedict has written the Lithuanian National Council of America that in response to its request he has ordered a collection next Sunday, May 20, in all Roman Catholic churches throughout the world for the relief of Lithuanians in the war.

• Chihuahua City, Mexico, May 18.—Official confirmation was received here today of a report that while the Namiquipa district Villa kidnaped 110 girls between the ages of 10 and 20 and kept them in his camp several weeks. Twenty of the girls are said to have died.

• New York, May 18.—Nikola Tesla, inventor, contributed more to the progress of electrical science during the year 1916 than any other man, the American Institute of Electrical Engineers decided at its annual meeting here tonight in awarding him the Edison medal.

• MADRID, via Paris, May 18.—A note of protest to Germany over the sinking of the Spanish steamer Pa[...] was drawn up at a cabinet meeting today presided over by King Alfonso.

"TRIBUNE" BEST NATIONAL PAPER, STUDENTS VOTE

New York, May 18.—[Special.]—Students in the senior class of the Pulitzer School of Journalism in Columbia university expressed their preferences regarding a number of things.

By the Australian ballot the students voted that THE CHICAGO TRIBUNE is the best national newspaper. Other "Bests" were:

Best author—H. G. Wells.
Best actor—Arnold Daly.
Best actress—Laurette Taylor.
Best poem—Oscar Wilde's "Ballad of Reading Gaol."
Best magazine—Saturday Evening Post.
Best Poet—Rudyard Kipling.

The school of journalism was founded by the late Joseph Pulitzer of the New York World.

Brazil Tires of Neutrality as U. S. Engages in War?

RIO DE JANEIRO, May 17.—[Special.]—It is believed that Brazil shortly revoke the decree of neutrality affecting the war between the United States and Germany.

6

A "Great Adventure" Begins

ON a foggy morning, May 28, the White Star Liner *Baltic* cast off her mooring lines and backed into the Hudson River. Aboard was General Pershing and his staff.

In his pocket were the parting orders from Secretary Baker, the crux of which appeared to be in one paragraph: . . . *the underlying idea must be kept in view that the forces of the United States are a separate and distinct component of the combined forces, the identity of which must be observed.*

"I shall give you only two orders, one to go and one to return," said Secretary of War Baker when he handed Pershing his papers, signed by the President, which made him absolute monarch of a military kingdom in Europe which he himself must create.

To a person of less determination and perseverance it might have seemed that he was supposed to raise an edifice built of bricks without straw. He knew that "the existing American Army was of no practical value," as General Peyton March said, for use in a European war. He knew that America had only 550 guns and enough ammunition to last through a nine-hour bombardment. The Flying Service counted 55 planes, 51 of which were obsolete and the other 4 obsolescent.

Joffre had stated flatly to his Allies that France did not have enough men of military age to replace their losses. A month earlier General Nivelle had attempted an offensive on the French front which had ended

The Yanks are coming. NATIONAL ARCHIVES

in a tragic fiasco followed by a mutiny which spread to 16 Army corps. The soldiers said they would defend their positions but would not advance. General Pétain replaced Nivelle. Thoroughly pessimistic but at least more realistic than his predecessor, he insisted that "we must wait for America and tanks." What the Allies expected from America was replacements, not an army.

Haig was more optimistic. He launched an offensive which, after a temporary and very limited success, was drowned in the mud of Flanders where it ended with terrible losses and a dangerous drop in morale.

The German blockade of Britain was having a devastating effect. One ship out of four which left British ports never returned. The German submarines seemed to be able to roam and kill at will. Jellicoe, British First Sea Lord, told Admiral Simms frankly when he arrived in London more than a month earlier: "It is impossible for us to go on with the war if losses like this continue." Britain's financial and economic resources were strained to the breaking point. And yet, not until forced to do so, would Jellicoe agree to the use of convoys, which he declared would be impractical. The first one tried on May 10 had been a success and by September the losses were drastically reduced.

But when Pershing crossed the Atlantic he was taking his chances with the rest.

Despite every manifest effort to compromise the secrecy of the sailing, capped by a booming salute from Governor's Island, the *Baltic* uneventfully navigated the U-boat-infested waters of the Atlantic. On June 8, to the accompanying chorus of a swarm of gulls, the transport pushed up the Mersey River toward Liverpool.

On the dock, the Royal Welch Fusiliers band stood like tin soldiers as they tooted through "God Save the King." Beside them, waiting for the distinguished American to disembark, was the official welcoming party and—dozens of newspapermen, for whom the General, partly through shyness, maintained admittedly "a natural aversion."

Floyd Gibbons, the American war correspondent, was among their number. The Chicago *Tribune* representative, who in February had survived the sinking of the *Laconia*, thought Pershing as well as his entire staff looked "lean, clean and keen."

Inspecting the honor guard after landing, Pershing asked one man, after a glance at an inconspicuous wound stripe:

"Where did you get your two wounds?"

The First Division arrives in St. Nazaire, June, 1917. One of the convoy's transports ties up preparatory to disembarking the first of the A.E.F. U. S. NAVY PHOTO

Pershing preceded his men to France by about two weeks. He is shown arriving at Boulogne with General Dumas. NATIONAL ARCHIVES

"At Givenchy and Lavenze, sir," replied the Tommy.

"You are a man," replied Pershing, and his reply sounded to Gibbons "sincere, all-meaning."

In London, the Commander-in-Chief of the A.E.F. was treated to a merry-go-round of receptions. At Buckingham Palace, the King pointed to the statue of Queen Victoria and observed indignantly to his American guest, apropos the Zeppelin raids:

"The Kaiser has even tried to destroy the statue of his own grandmother!"

Pershing, with his "grim sense of humor," thought this remark very droll.

England was but an interlude. The General had to get on with his journey. On June 13, he said goodbye to Ambassador Walter Hines Page as well as his British hosts, and left for the Channel steamer to Boulogne.

In the French seaport, Floyd Gibbons was again on hand to cover the Commander-in-Chief's arrival. He entrained with him to Paris the same afternoon, and then wrote of the welcome in the French capital:

> The sooty girders of the Gare du Nord shook with cheers when the special train pulled in . . . flashlights boomed and the Garde Républicain blared forth the strains of the "Star-Spangled Banner," bringing all the military to a halt and a long standing salute. It was followed by the "Marseillaise.". . .
>
> The crowds overflowed the sidewalks. They extended from the building walls out beyond the curbs and into the streets, leaving but a narrow lane through which the motors pressed their way slowly and with the exercise of much care. From the crowded balconies and windows overlooking the route, women and children tossed down showers of flowers and bits of colored paper.
>
> The crowds were so dense that other street traffic became marooned in the dense sea of joyously excited and gesticulating French people. Vehicles thus marooned immediately became islands of vantage. They were soon covered with men and women and children, who climbed on top of them and clung to the sides to get a better look at the khaki-clad occupants of the autos.
>
> Old gray-haired fathers of French fighting men bared their heads and with tears streaming down their cheeks shouted greetings to the tall, thin, gray-mustached American commander who was leading new armies to the support of their sons. Women heaped

armfuls of roses into the General's car and into the cars of other American officers who followed him, Paris street gamins climbed the lamp posts and waved their caps and wooden shoes and shouted shrilly.

Collier's Magazine editorialized:

When "Black Jack" Pershing strode down the gangplank at Boulogne to take command of our country's armed forces in France, a new volume was opened, a volume that may conceivably close with nothing less than the federation of the world.

That evening before the Crillon Hotel, jamming in the Place de la Concorde, pathetically grateful Parisians kept shouting for Pershing. America, at last, was coming to save them. Obligingly, he appeared and reappeared to wave from the balcony jutting out from his room.

The demonstration clashed with the Commander-in-Chief's personality and his passion for toiling in the background, anonymously, though such was now manifestly denied him. A parody, hurriedly scribbled, eloquently mirrored what Pershing so sincerely labeled "foolishness":

Oh, to be in Paris now that Pershing's there!
To hear the waves of welcome that greet him everywhere;
To see the children and the girls a-pelting him with flowers,
And feel that every petal is meant for us and ours. . . .

More circumspectly, the London *Daily Mail* wrote:

Although usually his aspect is rather serious he does not allow the heavy responsibilities imposed upon him to depress him. At the slightest provocation, his lips part in a smile and we understand then that the General can at times be exceedingly amiable.

John Pershing, however, wished only to dispense with official acclaim and get on with his mountainous responsibilities. He established headquarters in a small stucco building at 31 rue Constantine, across from Les Invalides—an office which would serve as a starter but obviously would be outgrown, to an uncomfortable degree, within weeks if not days.

As a residence, he was loaned the Louis XV château of Ogden

Mills, former Secretary of the Treasury, on the rue de Varenne. This charming estate held a further advantage for its cavalryman guest since it bordered on the Bois de Boulogne, enabling him to take morning and evening horseback rides.

In the whirlwind two weeks remaining of June, Pershing made a fast tour of the front near St. Quentin, commenced preliminary discussions with the French general staff on the role of the A.E.F., and proposed initially his plan for cracking through the Western Front: the elimination of the St. Mihiel salient, a bulge in the Hindenburg Line south of Verdun.

He at least earned the flattery already applied to him: "Go-getter Pershing."

On June 28 he was in St. Nazaire, greeting the first doughboys: those of the First Division. The Americans, such as they were, had arrived.

"They did not know how to keep step," observed Major Frederick Palmer, Pershing's press censor and former correspondent, "and which is the business end of a rifle and that when you march in a column of fours this does not mean three's and two's."

Conceding "the untrained, awkward appearance" of the soldiers, Pershing nonetheless was proud of this sampling of the A.E.F. The nucleus of the troops, in fact, had served with him on the Mexican border, a few of them in the Philippines. The two infantry brigades were commanded by his good friends Bullard and Brigadier General Omar Bundy.

All of these soldiers had been dubbed "Pershing's darlings." And the Commander-in-Chief did not dispute the sobriquet.

The British humor magazine *Punch* had its own way of summing up the impact of the A.E.F.'s arrival. With reference to the 1914 slurs upon Lord Kitchener's original British Expeditionary Force, a cartoonist depicted the Crown Prince imploring the Kaiser:

"For Gott's sake, Father, be careful this time—don't call the American army 'contemptible'!"

It was not, however, uncommon for some war-worn Tommies to make remarks about our "Eleventh Hour" soldiers.

The first of July found Pershing back in Paris. The pace was giddy and there was confusion aplenty. Due at Le Bourget flying field to congratulate a French ace, the Commander-in-Chief decided at the last minute to cancel this appearance.

The Commander-in-Chief of the A.E.F. at the tomb of Lafayette, Paris, July 4, 1917. NATIONAL ARCHIVES

Major Hugh A. Bayne of his staff, however, had not been informed. He arrived at Le Bourget in one of the staff cars with Old Glory and the General's stars plastered prominently upon it.

"As I descended from the automobile," Bayne reported, "the officer in command stepped forward and saluted. He was accompanied by a young aviator, dressed in red breeches and a light blue jacket, whom he presented, informing me that this hero had downed German *avions* and that he would have the honor of guiding me over the field. The youth's face shone with pride and joy as he took me in charge. Not another American officer had appeared.

"It dawned on me that there was a mistake somewhere. When, a moment later, the young man answered a question I asked by 'Oui, mon Général,' my suspicions were confirmed.

"But I realized that to reveal my identity to the boy would not only be a blow to his pride, but would create an awkward situation all around and that, even assuming that his captain eventually might learn the truth, he could be depended upon to hold his tongue lest he become the laughing stock of the French Army.

"So I decided to bow to the circumstances which were making me, for the time being, the Commander-in-Chief of the American Expeditionary Forces.

"When the tour of inspection was finished, I graciously thanked my guide and, pointing to the medal of the Legion of Honor on his chest, said, 'They tell me that your valor has well merited this honor.' He blushed with appreciation."

Bayne and the French officer with him, who happened to be a personal friend, had a good laugh on their drive back to Paris. He then told the French officer of a German general who died, so the story went, some years back at the house of an aunt in a little village. The aunt, by happenstance, died the next day, and plans were rushed to send the general's body back to Berlin and bury the little old lady in the village cemetery.

"Two days after the general's coffin had been shipped," Bayne narrated as their car drove on toward Paris, "the aunt's relatives took a last look into her coffin and found that, by mistake, the general, not the aunt, was in it! A telegram announcing this fact was immediately sent to the war department in Berlin.

"The answer came back, 'Aunt interred today with full military honors. Say nothing and bury the general in the village church yard."

So, Bayne concluded, he felt like the maiden aunt who had received the honors intended for the general.

The whole incident became, in turn, one of Pershing's favorite stories.

On July 4, Paris turned out to greet the doughboys. Chosen to parade through the city was the Second Battalion of the First Division's 16th Infantry Regiment. Pershing wrote of the tumultuous ovation:

". . . the battalion was joined by a great crowd, many women forcing their way into the ranks and swinging along arm in arm with the men. With wreaths about their necks and bouquets in their hats and rifles, the column looked like a moving flower garden. With only a semblance of military formation, the animated throng pushed its way through avenues of people to the martial strains of the French band and the still more thrilling music of cheering voices."

Pershing, astride his horse, had to gallop down parallel streets to keep ahead of the multitudes and ultimately reach the morning's destination: Picpus Cemetery in the Porte de Charenton section of Paris and the burial place of the Marquis de Lafayette.

The Commander-in-Chief stood by the tomb as an aide from the Quartermaster Corps, Colonel Charles E. Stanton, saluted and then solemnly proclaimed:

"Lafayette, we are here!"

7

"Hardship Will Be
Your Lot . . ."

PERSHING drove himself unmercifully that warm, rainy summer. His day started when the sun was barely peeking over the great metropolis' terra-cotta rooftops and the honk-honk of seemingly a million taxicabs was but a faint woodwind, the muted first notes of the day's overture.

He ate a very light breakfast—two soft-boiled eggs and a cup of black coffee—then galloped along the bridle paths. By Parisian standards, he was at his office on the rue Constantine at a ridiculously early hour. Facing him was an uncompromising accumulation of paper work and usually an anteroom packed with callers.

In a very short time, the Commander-in-Chief realized, he must assess the situation on the Western Front and the immediate needs of the Allies. Already he was convinced that "France is very tired of this war" and that "disaster" could be lurking on the spring's horizon.

He believed that a minimum expeditionary force of one million men should be in France by May, and one far better trained than the first sampling. It should, moreover, be staffed with officers "in full mental and physical vigor."

Although he preferred, as a general thing, to deal with newspapers through Major Palmer, he nonetheless granted the Associated Press an interview with the primary purpose of telling the home front some of the hard imponderables of the war:

67

There was always something to do. Pershing, with Major General Summerall, inspects the First Division. NATIONAL ARCHIVES

Those of us who have fully studied the situation and who know what is necessary to be done are anxious that the people at home shall strive to realize the immensity of the task in which we are engaged and shall, through patience and confidence, help us to accomplish that task in the shortest possible time. Everything is going well with us, both as a nation and as an army. We are making giant strides day by day but we are just started.

We came into this war without an army—so now we must build an entire organization. . . .

It is impossible to create a vast fighting machine merely by the wave of the hand . . . until we can properly take our place in the line the people must be patient and as confident as we are, who know what we are doing and what we must do.

Those of his staff such as Colonel Charles G. Dawes, the A.E.F.'s general purchasing agent, were already filled with an uncustomary hero worship.

"Pershing," Dawes wrote in his diary, "is the man for this great

The Commander-in-Chief addresses the officers of the First Division.
NATIONAL ARCHIVES

emergency. He has an immense faculty for disposing of things. He is not only a great soldier, but he has great common sense and tremendous energy."

Dawes had lost his son in an accident. The 21-year-old Rufus Fearing Dawes had been drowned in Lake Geneva in 1912, and the mutual loss created its own bond between the two outwardly formidable officers.

"We have both passed through the greatest grief which can come to man," Dawes avowed. "As we rode together there occurred an instance of telepathy which was too much for either of us. Neither of us was saying anything, but I was thinking of my lost boy and of John's loss and looking out of the window, and he was doing the same thing on the other side of the automobile. We both turned at the same time and each was in tears. All John said was, 'Even this war can't keep it out of my mind.'"

Felix Frankfurter, the lawyer, having completed a special mission in France for Secretary Baker, reported with comparable enthusiasm upon the Commander-in-Chief:

"General Pershing impressed me as in the grip of a responsibility, the truly awful nature of which he thoroughly understands. He is full of burning but calm determination, has a hopeful sense of humility as to his personal relation to the task and is fully mindful of the fact that he is entrusted with the fate of a large portion of the youth of America and the anxieties of their families, mindful also that he is the symbol and the agent of the great purpose which the United States has avowed to the world.

"There is an atmosphere of simple directness about our headquarters in Paris. The members of the General Staff with whom I came in contact were themselves convincing proof of their statement that the General Staff on the whole are competent, are living in a spirit of hard work and with a serious realization of the magnitude of the problems they will be increasingly called upon to solve."

Almost every evening, Pershing somehow found the time to be tutored in French. A poor linguist, halting in self-expression even in his native tongue, the Missourian nonetheless pursued the study of French

Pershing, with Major General James G. Harbord (*second from right*), **grits his teeth to listen to a concert of the Republican Guard Band.**
NATIONAL ARCHIVES

with the same dogged determination characteristic of his ministrations toward the embryo A.E.F.

His struggle with the French language and his feeling of compulsion which goaded him to take it up in the first place were but lesser facets of "the truly awful nature" of Pershing's responsibility. Bumbling and inefficiency on the part of members of that euphemistic anomaly, "the war team," was another torment of mushrooming stature.

He was finally forced to cable the War Department: RECOMMEND NO FURTHER SHIPMENTS BE MADE OF FOLLOWING ARTICLES: BATH BRICKS, BOOKCASES, BATHTUBS, CABINETS FOR BLANKS, CHAIRS EXCEPT FOLDING CHAIRS, CUSPIDORS, OFFICE DESKS, FLOOR WAX, HOSE EXCEPT FIRE HOSE, STEPLADDERS, LAWN MOWERS . . .

His task was overflowing the limitations of his rue Constantine headquarters. In the early fall, Pershing moved to Chaumont, a beautiful town in the hills of eastern France, and at the gateway to Lorraine as well as the broad front extending from Toul to Verdun.

As an A.E.F. headquarters, it was especially suitable since there was a large French army caserne ready for the American staffers to provide living and working space. The Commander-in-Chief himself took up residence in a storybook castle four miles south of Chaumont, known as the Château Val des Escoliers. He never learned how to spell its name, much less pronounce it, but it was more than adequate for working, entertaining and—living. The woodland paths snaking away from its every side afforded an opportunity for pleasurable riding such as Pershing had not known since his days with the Sixth Cavalry.

Soon Chaumont became the mecca for Allied general staff officers, for missions from the States, sightseeing congressmen, for civilian visitors of every business, profession and personal whim or inclination.

One of them, William Allen White, a Kansas editor, noted:

He breathes confidence in him into people's hearts. He never seems confidential though he is entirely cordial. Again one feels sure that there is no court around him. He seems wise with his own wisdom, which is constantly in touch with the wisdom of every one who may have business with him.

At Gondrecourt, a two hours' drive through the Meuse valley, the Commander-in-Chief kept check on the First Division, under training by the French. Like a mother hen, he watched over his soldiers, goaded, praised and often scolded them. He further clinched his well-established reputation for being able to spot a missing or unfastened button amidst columns of thousands of men.

In October, the officer who, to some, seemed exaggeratedly concerned over buttons and other trivialities, was promoted to a four-star general, a rank previously held only by Washington, Grant, Sherman and Sheridan.

The next month, the A.E.F. counted its first casualties. Going into the trenches northeast of Nancy to hold its first sector, the 16th Infantry of the First Division was assaulted in a probing but fierce trench raid. Three Americans were killed, five wounded and twelve taken prisoner by the Germans.

On November 30, a detachment of the 11th Regiment of Engineers, with a similar number of Canadian counterparts, was working on the railway yards at Gouzeaucourt, in the British Cambrai sector. A major railway junction, Cambrai appeared to be firmly in the hands of the Germans. All efforts to recapture it had been bloodily repulsed.

Late in the afternoon, the Germans in force poured from the Moeuvres and Bourlon woods and virtually surrounded the Allies. Trap-

Scattered units of the A.E.F. infantry and artillery went into action in French and British sectors late in 1917. NATIONAL ARCHIVES

On the eastern side of the Western Front, Marshal Hindenburg
(*extreme left foreground*) was as busy as his opponent, Pershing. In
the center is the Kaiser. They are walking through a captured
French town. NATIONAL ARCHIVES

ped at their construction work, the Americans fought back with shovels
and spades in this unequal engagement.

Six of the doughboys were killed, still more wounded and captured
before further resistance was deemed folly. The British paid heavily,
losing 4,000 prisoners.

"There they stood before us," one of the German officers was quoted
in the Berlin press, "these young men from the land of liberty. They were
sturdy and sportsmanlike in build. Good-natured smiles radiated from
their blue eyes. . . ."

Pershing, while acclaiming the valor of his engineers, knew that this
was not soldiering. A war, in the twentieth century, would never be won
by troops wielding shovels.

The Yanks move up from training areas through a ruined village.
NATIONAL ARCHIVES

The doughboys learn how to advance under cover of a giant English
tank. NATIONAL ARCHIVES

All quiet on the Western Front.
An American listening post. U. S. ARMY

The little children of Chaumont have brought the American general flowers. NATIONAL ARCHIVES

Too, it would only be won by the utmost co-ordination and confidence among the Allies. General Pershing could not forget his role, toward this end, as diplomat as well as military leader. On December 8, for example, he wrote to Brigadier General W. W. Atterbury, former vice-president of the Pennsylvania Railroad and now Director General of Transportation:

"With reference to our conversation the other day regarding the Belgian engines, it seemed to me that you were not very much impressed with the fact that they had been secured. I am not quite of that opinion but believe that when the matter is fully investigated we shall find it to be a very great saving in transportation to ourselves and to the French and British as well. At any rate, I ordered it done and that is sufficient.

"In any event the engines have been turned over to us by the Belgians in the belief that they were doing us a favor, so that I think every advantage should be taken of this fact and that every assurance should be given to them that they have done us a favor, and we should be careful that nothing to the contrary reaches them in an official or unofficial way. . . .

The Commander-in-Chief horseback riding near his château headquarters, Chaumont. NATIONAL ARCHIVES

"With reference to another matter which the French are making some adverse comments about, that is a lengthy visit to M. Clemenceau. Usually when any matter assumes the importance of an interview with the Prime Minister himself, it should be brought to my attention and the matter be taken up by me. . . . I appreciate your eagerness to get things accomplished and your efficiency in your work, but we must, as far as possible, be governed by every consideration of custom and diplomacy in dealing with the French people, especially with those in high position."

Avery Andrews, classmate of Pershing's at West Point, had returned from civilian life to duty as a colonel in the Engineers. This December he arrived at Chaumont, where he was instantly impressed with the Commander-in-Chief's productive capacity and "with the amount of time and study . . . to organization problems, and particularly to those relating to the General Staff. He said that when he first organized his headquarters in France, then very small, he tried to write or correct every important letter or cable; and did so until he felt sufficient confidence in his staff to delegate to them much of the routine work."

Nonetheless, with a do-or-die resolve, Pershing was determined to keep healthy. One December morning Colonel Dawes, a regular visitor at Chaumont, looked out of the window of the château and witnessed a remarkable sight:

". . . There was 'Black Jack' clad only in pajamas running up and down in the snow outdoors. I never saw a man more physically fit at his age."

The same month, clothing figured in another day of Pershing's activity. Accompanying Sir Douglas Haig, commander of the B.E.F., he was on a visit to King Albert of the Belgians at Adinkerke, near Boulogne. The train, to Pershing's dismay, arrived 10 minutes early.

"I was very incompletely dressed when it stopped," wrote Pershing, "and I found that the King of the Belgians was at the station with an escort band playing the 'Star-Spangled Banner.' I kept him waiting a few minutes, but I did dress rapidly. Went with the King by motor to a little château just inside of Belgium, near Houthem.

The Missouri-born Pershing was little impressed by royalty. He confided in his diary after King George V reviewed American troops, that what a king thinks "will have very little influence on the situation." NATIONAL ARCHIVES

(*Left*) **Pershing and the hero of Verdun, General Joseph "Papa" Joffre.**
(*Right*) **Pershing and the Supreme Allied Commander, Marshal Foch.**
NATIONAL ARCHIVES

"The King took me in and presented me to the Queen before I got my overcoat off. I thought they seemed about as ill at ease as [Captain Carl] Boyd and myself. Stayed there for luncheon. At luncheon, matters eased up considerably when they got me to speaking French; in fact the conversation became quite gay. The King and Queen were most hospitable."

Among other duties expected of him was the reviewing of French troops who had distinguished themselves in action. Returning from Houthem, he paused for such an occasion. During the ceremonies a French boy, disheveled and dirty, squirmed through the crowd along the street, on his hands and feet.

Finally, within range of General Pershing, he waved a tattered fragment of an American flag and shouted, "Vive Pershing!"

The Commander-in-Chief wheeled to face the lad and came to a stiff, formal salute, without the trace of a grin. As one spectator observed, "He look like ze statue carve out of stone."

A few days later, a little girl broke through another group of townspeople to hand Pershing a bouquet. Somehow, the General was always ill at ease holding floral tributes.

Heywood Broun, a correspondent, remarked of Pershing's reaction when handling flowers: "The holding of them was much as a doughboy might hold his first armful of live grenades."

. . . Now the year 1917 was ending, the year in which America went "over there." Christmas would be spent by tens of thousands of its young citizens in strange surroundings in a strange, distant and imperiled land.

To Pershing it was a time of penetrating loneliness, a season when once again he would naturally think of Frances and of his little girls, Helen Elizabeth, Anne, and Mary, who in the sweep and enigma of time would never, never come back to him—no more than could the last Christmas tree he had shared with them, the tinsel, the cotton balls and the toys at the base.

His family and all of the keepsakes which had once—and so ephemerally—been associated with his family were as lost to his conscious world of reality as though they had never existed at all other than in some fancy and caprice of his mind.

Pershing, however, had never lost the faith and the courage that his mother and his Methodist Sunday school teachers had helped to plant within him, long ago.

He wrote, in a Christmas message to his troops:

> *Hardship will be your lot but trust in God will give you comfort; temptation will befall you, but the teachings of our Saviour will give you strength. Let your valor as a soldier and your conduct as a man be an inspiration to your comrades and an honor to your country— Germany can be beaten, Germany must be beaten, Germany will be beaten!*

8

Rendezvous

THE new year, 1918, started out in the United States with record-breaking cold and snowstorms. In New York City, the thermometer sank to 13° below zero, the coldest ever recorded on Manhattan Island.

The weather, however, did not chill the ardor of the wartime dreams of Americans.

"It will be a knightly army," impassionedly declared Secretary of War Baker, "not an army of conquest that expects to come home with a chariot and somebody chained to the wheels and loaded with material spoils, but an army that is going over to live and die for the fine fruits of a high idealism and a purified national morality."

From the blizzard-swept plains of Kansas, its governor, Arthur Capper, wrote in similar vein to Chaumont's most distinguished guest:

"It has gladdened the hearts of Kansas people to learn you have taken precautions to insure the sobriety and high moral standard of the American troops under your command in France. We learn you have forbidden the use of strong liquors and have under consideration the exclusion of all alcoholic beverages. We have heard also that the protection of our troops from immorality begins the moment they land and that you have declared places of evil repute 'off the limits' of the camps and have prohibited their visitation by members of the American Expeditionary Forces. . . . We are anxious that our Kansas boys who go to the front to fight for world freedom shall be made just as secure from the preying influence of liquor, vice and immorality after they land in France as they were in their home communities.

"So I voice a prayer of thanks to you from thousands of grateful fathers and mothers in Kansas for your noble endeavor to place about them a cloak of protection and to render them still more fit for the moral and the physical fight they must make."

Pershing had provided further fuel to the social reformers, to the morality-leaguers, to the stiff-collar church workers and the do-gooders of many visages by banning the Soldiers' Godmothers' League—an organization to promote correspondence from the trenches. Soldiers, the Commander-in-Chief ruled, shouldn't be writing to "strange women."

Thus, an iron-bound buttress may have been wished and legislated into position around the soldiers' morals. But in other respects, the war effort was proving less effective.

The chief problem for some Americans which the European war had created was how to keep out of it. Certainly from the Alleghenies to the Rockies there was a strong sentiment in favor of holding the hand to the plow and the eye on the furrow; the East was less neutral, but when the first call for enlistments came it was the Middle West which made the greatest voluntary contribution. But that wasn't enough. Then came the Draft, which met with little or no opposition but was delayed because of lack of shelter and supplies. Housing for such a force (the first draft called for a million) was nonexistent. Butchers, bakers and candle-stick makers were soon building leaky barracks for double the money they could earn with cleaver or shaving brush. The construction was bad enough but it wasn't fast enough.

The Army borrowed a few thousand blankets from the Navy. Sheets came back from the laundry metamorphosed into cheesecloth. Troops shivered in cotton shorts and khaki while sheep blatted to be shorn.

Next to trained men to fill the ranks the greatest need was officers. Training camps were formed producing the "Ninety-Day Wonders," mostly drawn from the colleges.

By the spring of 1918, 57,000 candidates had received commissions.

The third problem was the most difficult to solve and it turned Pershing gray: supplies. Without preparation, a switch from peace to war production took time. Obtaining the transportation facilities was a colossal task.

The Quartermaster Corps, which had been a target of some of Pershing's sharpest criticism, was still doing nothing to disprove a thesis that at least some of its officers must be stark-raving mad. Among their indiscretions, the officers had purchased 945,000 saddles and 2,800,000 bridles and halters for a cavalry pegged at approximately an 86,000-horse strength. They were probably thinking in terms of a war with Mexico and merely using the multiplication table.

As if to compound this irrationality, 86,000 pounds of copper, at 39½ cents a pound, were earmarked for branding irons. This would average about two branding irons per horse.

In France, where the weather was as cold and snowy as in the United States, the confusion in initial planning and logistics was equaled by the ineptitude of the officers themselves. General Von Stein, the Kaiser's Minister of War, had taunted that "sewing epaulettes on American uniforms did not make officers of them!"

Pershing, inclined to agree with the criticism, advised the War Department of "an almost total failure to give instruction in principles of minor tactics and their practical application to war conditions. Officers, from colonels down, and including some general officers, are found ignorant of the handling of units in open warfare, including principles of reconnaissance, outposts, advance guard, solution of practical problems, and formation of attack."

Nor was there much to cheer him in his deteriorating relationships with his Allies. The French, as Pershing confided to his staff, "were dead set on getting our troops under their control." The English had almost identical designs.

He cabled Washington: THE FRENCH HAVE NOT BEEN ENTIRELY FRANK, AS UNOFFICIAL INFORMATION INDICATES THEY REALLY WANT TO INCORPORATE OUR REGIMENTS INTO THEIR DIVISIONS FOR SUCH SERVICES AS THEY DESIRE. . . . THE INTEGRITY OF OUR FORCES SHOULD BE PRESERVED AS FAR AS POSSIBLE.

Pershing had a clearer view of the future, perhaps because he had not been for long too near the woods to see the trees. He told Generalissimo Foch, the Supreme Allied Commander with whom he was drawn into almost continual wrangling, "The time may come when the American Army will have to stand the brunt of this war, and it is not wise to fritter away our resources. . . . It would be a grave mistake to give up the idea of building an American Army in all its details as rapidly as possible."

The winter continued, as the exact part to be played by the A.E.F. remained entirely uncertain. In their training areas scattered along the

There were horses and mules in the A.E.F., as this photograph attests, but surely not sufficient for the nearly 3 million bridles and halters some addled Quartermaster Corps purchasing agent had secured. NATIONAL ARCHIVES

Doughboys learning trench raiding, in a section of no man's land, near Badonviller, March, 1918. NATIONAL ARCHIVES

Aircraft production in the United States just couldn't get off the ground. American fliers had to use French and English machines. This is a light Breguet bomber of the 96th Aero Squadron, taking off from Amanty.

eastern French countryside, just behind the lines, the men alternately shivered in their billets and miserable makeshift barracks and drilled in mock-up trenches, preparing for a war which was to be fought in the open.

Pershing's diary chronicled matters both great and not so great. On February 4, for example, he wrote:

"At Paris, worked in quarters in morning. Saw General Russell. Took General [Peyton] March to call on General Foch and M. Clemenceau. Lunched with Noon Day Club. Took Colonel Andrews with me. Had photographs made at Waliry, 9-bis rue de Landres. Saw Colonel Webb C. Hayes. Went to see Dr. Borsch to have glasses adjusted. Dined with Colonel Dawes, Colonel [James L.] Collins, Colonel and Mrs. Boyd at Ritz."

There were other hazards in wartime besides enemy action. On February 10, while inspecting the Second Division, he noted, "I sprained a tendon in the calf of my leg and returned to headquarters, leaving General [James G.] Harbord to continue the inspection."

Harbord was Chief of Staff.

A week later, the tendon healed, Pershing was back inspecting with vigor, and some anger, for he was always concerned for the sick and wounded. He wrote, on February 18:

"Went to Vittel where I visited Base Hospital No. 36 under command of Major Philippe: Major Rukke being in command at the town. The place was dirty and it was very evident that the discipline was poor. The same remarks apply to Base Hospital No. 31 at Contrexeville, where Major Schlanser was in command. Stopped next at Bournonne-les-Bains where I saw the headquarters of the 3d Cavalry, Colonel Beach commanding, billets of machine gun troop in small hotel in the town and headquarters and master corrals. The regiment gave evidence of slack management from every point of view. It is also in need of equipment. . . . Visited detachment of 26th Engineers at Montigny-le-Roc, in command of Captain Chambers. Men going about the street presented a very slovenly appearance. Captain Chambers was directed to give them one-hour's drill per day. Arrived at Chaumont at about 6 P.M."

Bad as things might have been, nonetheless, Pershing did not want evangelists such as Billy Sunday to come over to try to straighten them out. He wrote to a friend in Washington who had inquired about sending the peppery preacher to France:

"I have very little time to keep in touch with affairs other than

One never knew when Pershing would show up. Colonel George E. Leach, of the Rainbow Division, for example, was descending from his hayloft billet at Baccarat when he almost literally tumbled onto the Commander-in-Chief. The General immediately asked "what I had done to prepare myself to be a colonel of a regiment of artillery. . . ." NATIONAL ARCHIVES

those of a military nature, but of course we have all heard of Billy Sunday and appreciate the great work he has undoubtedly done in the United States.

"Conditions in Europe, however, are different, and so far as creating enthusiasm among our soldiers is concerned, I feel that the morale of the Army is now and always will be maintained on a very high plane. Everyone who visits the Army in France is impressed with its morale and that the nearer you get to the trenches the higher it is."

By mid-March it became all too apparent that Ludendorff would strike, especially since Foch showed no inclination to mount a spring offensive. On March 21, the great drive thundered into life on a flaming sector all the way from Arras to La Fere, with the goal, quite possibly, the capture of the Channel ports and the paralysis of the British Army and, once again, the outflanking of Paris from the north—separating the Allied forces.

In the initial 5-hour bombardment, more shells were expended than in the whole Franco-Prussian War.

Minister of War Lord Derby sent an urgent cable from London to his country's ambassador in Washington, Lord Reading:

"We have every hope of checking him, but our losses have been very heavy, and will be heavier . . ." Captured Germans filing past wounded Yanks. NATIONAL ARCHIVES

"But I've a rendezvous with death. . . ." AMERICAN RED CROSS

WE HAVE EVERY HOPE OF CHECKING HIM, BUT OUR LOSSES HAVE
BEEN VERY HEAVY AND WILL BE HEAVIER. THIS IS ONLY THE BEGINNING
OF THE CAMPAIGN OF 1918 AND WE HAVE TO LOOK TO THE FUTURE. IN
THE PRESENT STATE OF OUR MANPOWER RESOURCE WE CANNOT KEEP
OUR DIVISIONS SUPPLIED WITH DRAFTS FOR MORE THAN A SHORT TIME
AT THE PRESENT RATE OF LOSS, AND WE SHALL BE HELPLESS TO AS-
SIST OUR ALLIES IF, AS IS VERY PROBABLE, THE ENEMY TURN AGAINST
THEM LATER. WE HAVE THE DIVISIONAL CADRES READY WITH ALL NEC-
ESSARY SERVICES, AND WHAT WE REQUIRE IS MEN TO HELP US KEEP
THEM FILLED. YOU SHOULD APPEAL TO PRESIDENT [Wilson] TO DROP
ALL QUESTIONS OF INTERPRETATION OF PAST AGREEMENTS AND SEND
OVER INFANTRY AS FAST AS POSSIBLE WITHOUT TRANSPORT OR OTHER
INCUMBRANCES.

THE SITUATION IS UNDOUBTEDLY CRITICAL AND IF AMERICA DELAYS
NOW SHE MAY BE TOO LATE.

On March 25, Pershing hurried to Marshal Pétain's headquarters at Compiègne. The former's diary recounted the dramatic sequence which followed:

"Arrived there about 10 P.M. General Pétain had changed houses since we were last there. At headquarters they left a guide who took us to his new abode. We found him, General Antoine, his Chief of Staff, General Raguenau and Commandant Cochet waiting for us. General Pétain had ready the map of the right of the French line where the American divisions had been serving.

"No time was wasted. Everyone talked fast; Cochet and Boyd both interpreted as rapidly as they could. I agreed to Pétain's urgent request that American divisions take their place as soon as possible in quiet sectors of the line so that French divisions might be relieved and sent to the

"M. Clemenceau showed a buoyancy and gleam of fire in his face that made me realize why they call him 'Le Tigre.' " NATIONAL ARCHIVES

The Commander-in-Chief ready to visit the front, and in an explosively gay mood behind the lines. NATIONAL ARCHIVES

battle. I had insisted that it be the policy to work toward the formation of an American Corps, and General Pétain agreed to this principle.

"Each of us agreed that it is not now the time to form this corps. General Pétain and I were in perfect agreement on all points."

Pershing spent the next three days in Paris, under bombardment by the Germans' long-range guns, then left to visit Foch at Clermont. Waiting in the garden of the French commander's well-guarded and well-hidden château, Pershing admired "a cherry tree in full bloom"; then continued his report:

". . . there was no sound in sight that would make one realize that not more than 30 kilometres to the northeast the French were at that moment counter-attacking furiously against Montdidier and to the east. This latter is the counter-attack which I had said to the Secretary of War a few hours before should in all probability take place.

"I soon went to see M. Clemenceau, General Foch, General Pétain and M. Lucheur. They explained the situation to me. M. Clemenceau and General Pétain went out in the yard and I said to General Foch what I had come to say, namely that we are ready and anxious for a chance to do our part in the fight and that I stood ready for any suggestion as to how we might help.

"Spring was returning to the earth . . ." U. S. ARMY PHOTOGRAPH

"General Foch was manifestly touched and insisted that we go at once to M. Clemenceau. We went into the garden and saw him and General Pétain standing in the gravel walk by a cedar tree. General Foch in his enthusiasm rushed across the lawn, holding me by the arm as he went. He told them quickly what I had to say. M. Clemenceau showed a buoyancy and gleam of fire in his face that made me realize why they call him 'Le Tigre.'

"General Pétain, who has a very unchangeable face and manner for a Frenchman, reflected the appreciation of his comrades. They were all manifestly touched. Under the inspiration of the moment, Boyd says I out-Frenched the French; that my subconscious mind came into play and that I spoke to them in their own language with words which I could not have commanded 10 minutes before or 10 minutes afterward."

It was a remarkable fruit of the long hours Pershing had spent learning his lessons. (Also, he admitted, probably slightly revised by the French who recorded it.)

"Je viens pour vous dire que le peuple américain tiendrait à grand honneur que nos troupes fussent engagés dans la présente bataille . . ." was how the Commander-in-Chief of the A.E.F. commenced. It was, he said, "a great honor" to consider placing the American troops in the present battle line. He added, "Infantry, artillery, aviation, all that we have is yours; use it as you wish. More will come, in numbers equal to requirements."

Later, Pershing ordered the First Division to be prepared for action. Soon he assembled their officers and delivered a fighting talk that inspired even the hardened, cynical war correspondents.

He spoke, noted Wilbur Forrest of the United Press, with "sweeping arm-length fist-clenched gestures," as he exhorted:

"You are going to meet savage enemies flushed with victory. Meet them like Americans! You are leading men. Be an inspiration to them! When you hit, hit hard and don't stop hitting. You don't know the meaning of the word defeat!"

It was now April. Spring was returning to the earth, even to the blasted, shell-pocked, devastated and gas-poisoned earth of France. The slaughter of last year, the year before and the year before that would certainly be repeated. As American soldiers clutched their rifles, at least some of them were mindful of Alan Seeger's prophetic verse:

> *I have a rendezvous with Death*
> *At some disputed barricade,*
> *When spring comes back with rustling shade*
> *And apple-blossoms fill the air . . .*

The doughboys found that village fighting was just like the stories they'd read about cowboys and Indians. NATIONAL ARCHIVES

9

Summer

APRIL and much of May passed without the A.E.F. tasting battle. The Germans did not outflank Paris nor did they destroy the British Army. Before their fury was partially contained, however, they had pounded to within 20 miles of Calais and swept the French and some English from their supposedly impregnable positions along the Chemin des Dames ridge.

The Allies were imperiled. Prime Ministers Clemenceau of France, Lloyd George of England, and Orlando of Italy, advised President Wilson that 162 Allied divisions were now trying to hold off 200 of the Central Powers, and there was "an immediate danger of an Allied defeat in the present campaign owing to the Allied reserves being exhausted before those of the enemy." The urgent cable continued:

> HE [Foch] PLACES THE TOTAL AMERICAN FORCE REQUIRED . . . AT NO LESS THAN 100 DIVISIONS, AND URGES THE CONTINUOUS RAISING OF FRESH AMERICAN LEVIES, WHICH, IN HIS OPINION, SHOULD NOT BE LESS THAN 300,000 A MONTH, WITH A VIEW TO ESTABLISHING A TOTAL AMERICAN FORCE OF 100 DIVISIONS AT AS EARLY A DATE AS THIS CAN POSSIBLY BE DONE.

Pershing, for all his offering "all that we have," would not yield an inch as far as giving up his purpose of creating an independent Army. On

April 25, Foch bluntly told the grim cavalryman that "the American Army may arrive to find the British pushed into the sea and the French driven back behind the Loire, while it tries in vain to organize on lost battlefields over the graves of Allied soldiers."

Pershing laconically replied that he was willing to take the risk. "I thought," he explained, "that the best and quickest way to help the Allies would be to build up an American Army."

At another emergency conference, called in Abbeville early in May before the expected and impending German drive on Soissons, Pershing faced Lloyd George, Clemenceau and Italian Premier Orlando. They asked in effect: "Can't you see that the war will be lost unless we get American manpower for replacements of losses in our own ranks which we can no longer furnish?"

Pershing remained unmoved. They continued to repeat their demands until, as he himself reported, "whereupon I struck the table with my fist and said with the greatest possible emphasis, 'Gentlemen, I have thought this programme over deliberately and we will not be coerced!' "

Routine was accelerated in the A.E.F., though there were those on Pershing's staff who would not have thought that possible. Everything was "rush!" "hurry!" "without delay!" Meetings were announced and expected to be in progress within five minutes or preferably less.

Three days later at Chaumont, General Foch and top French Army advisers met with Pershing and agreed on a *modus operandi* for victory which the generals thought would come in 1919.

". . . We must have 80 American divisions in France by April and 100 by July of that year. It was also agreed that General Foch should send a cable to President Wilson informing him that he learns that the Germans are withdrawing some divisions from Russia to be sent to the Western Front."

On May 28, one division of the A.E.F. at last went into full-scale action. General Bullard's First Division captured Cantigny, a village 50 miles north of Paris, the key to a small but important salient between Paris and Amiens. The Commander-in-Chief noted proudly that "our troops behaved splendidly and suffered but slight loss. It had an excellent effect on morale—both the Allies' and our own."

Two days later came Château-Thierry, and then in a week, Belleau Wood, Vaux, Lucy-le-Bocage and other villages which became monuments to American achievement. For the second time in the war, a wall of defenders had blocked the road to Paris.

After four years of war, these Tommies were understandably weary.
NATIONAL ARCHIVES

By midsummer the A.E.F., overseas, was a million strong, and a quarter of that total was in action. U. S. ARMY PHOTOGRAPH

The Germans had hurled thirty divisions against the French line, captured Soissons and pushed a great salient southward, investing Château-Thierry which straddles the great Metz-Paris highway, the Chemin-des-Dames. A part of the town occupies the southern bank of the Marne.

The enemy was now within 49 miles of Paris, heading toward a relatively flat country with no natural obstacles before it and only dead-tired French troops, backed by almost as battle-weary reserves, between them and the capital.

The 7th Machine Gun Battalion, of the Third Division, one of the few such completely motorized, was the first to arrive at the bridgehead at Château-Thierry. It did so after a forced overnight journey from its encampment at Le Ferté-sur-Aube, 100 kilometers distant.

In a wild two days' "cowboys-and-Indians" kind of battle the machine gunners, reinforced by French Moroccans, and by the American Second Division, held the Germans on the other side of the river.

The bulge in the line was effectively shored up.

Echoes of the battle of Château-Thierry had hardly died when the French were forced to call again upon the Americans. To the northwest

The big parade. NATIONAL ARCHIVES

of Château-Thierry the French, completely worn out fighting a rear-guard action, were retreating westward along the valley of the Marne. The Second A.E.F. Division, which included one brigade of Marines, answered the call.

The Germans didn't know that Americans were replacing the exhausted French. Naturally, they were confused when a retreating enemy suddenly began aggressive resistance. The battle of Belleau Wood and Vaux became history. The sacrifice in losses was great. But it was worth it. Again a human wall stood immovable between the enemy and Paris.

Pershing commented:

"The German lines were favorably located on commanding ground and were made more formidable by the extensive use of machine guns. . . . The success . . . was obtained with but little assistance from the tired French divisions on its flanks."

About this time, Brigadier General John A. Lejeune, a Marine Corps veteran of Cuba, the Philippines and Vera Cruz, arrived in France and reported to Chaumont. He hoped that Pershing would give him a brigade of his own.

"We had a very good dinner and the General was most agreeable," Lejeune wrote to his wife that evening. "He has simple, unaffected manners and was most informal and affable. He looks well but sad. He bears a great responsibility that no one can share with him, and carries besides a heavy burden of personal sorrow."

During the conversation the Commander-in-Chief "expressed the deepest sorrow" over the casualties at Belleau Wood.

". . . his voice broke and he showed deep emotion, so much so that one of the members of his staff said, 'We must remember, General, that Napoleon said that it is just as impossible to win victories without loss of life as it is to make omelets without breaking eggs.'"

For the moment, however, Pershing did not give his friend Lejeune a command.

Two other visitors, of contrasting personalities, arrived shortly after Lejeune: Elsie Janis, the petite entertainer, and Walter Damrosch, the conductor.

When Pershing shook hands with Elsie, whose *"spécialité de la maison"* was turning cartwheels on the tail gate of Army trucks, it seemed to her that the "famous smile" broke suddenly "like sunshine after rain above his strong chin." He told her:

"I'm delighted to meet you. I suppose I may call you Elsie as all the men do?"

She thought to herself that she would like to reply, "Call me anything you like, Jack." Instead, she answered demurely: "Yes, sir."

After she had sung "Over There," "The Long, Long Trail" and the rest of the A.E.F. favorites for an assemblage of doughboys, Pershing complimented her:

"Elsie, when you first came to France someone said you were more valuable than an entire regiment, then someone raised it to a division, but I want to tell you that if you can give our men this sort of happiness, you are worth an Army Corps."

He provided her with a khaki-colored Cadillac, with Army chauffeur and headquarters stars on the radiator grille, and unlimited frontline and restricted-area passes—all to be used as long as she was in France.

The eminent conductor, Damrosch, was traveling in France with a semivague purpose as president of the war-born American Friends of Musicians in France.

As Damrosch certainly expected, the Commander-in-Chief invited

Elsie Janis toured the front lines, was again under fire in Paris during its shelling and, as final penance, caught a touch of the flu. She delighted the boys by turning cartwheels as she sang. NATIONAL ARCHIVES

"Whippet" tanks going forward near Boureuilles, September 26, 1918, at the opening of the Meuse-Argonne drive. NATIONAL ARCHIVES

(*Left*) **Advance in the Argonne under donkey power.** NATIONAL ARCHIVES

(*Right*) **Gas mask drill was awfully funny to some soldiers.** NATIONAL ARCHIVES

him to dinner—a host the man of music considered "soldierly, dignified, courteous and simple in his bearing, wearing a uniform as only a man can who has been a soldier all his life."

Pershing confided to Damrosch that he had never thought the American military bands could compare with those of, say, France and England. He wondered what could be done to improve the quality.

The conductor pointed out that one important consideration was increasing the stature of a bandsman in military tables of organization. He had noted, for example, that musicians frequently were assigned as stretcher-bearers, a job requiring but rudimentary skill.

The next morning, Damrosch was immensely gratified when an officer-escort, smiling, handed him a copy of a new order to the effect that "from now on bandsmen are not to be used any longer as stretcher-bearers except in cases of extreme military emergency."

It was as though Damrosch had introduced a phase of human accomplishment new to the Commander-in-Chief, and he reacted with characteristic enthusiasm. For one thing, he would order military bandmasters to Paris in groups of 50 a week, where the American conductor would "test their efficiency."

By and large, however, the reason for music and musicians all added up to one familiar conclusion in Pershing's mind, as he observed with warmth to Walter Damrosch:

"When peace is declared and our bands march up Fifth Avenue I should like them to play so well that it will be another proof of the advantage of military training."

More and more American soldiers were pouring into France. Now the A.E.F. was nearly a million strong.

One of the recent arrivals was the 78th Division, which was ordered to stand inspection by the Commander-in-Chief almost before the troops had fully made the transition from ship to shore. As one of its members, who signed himself "Private Alden," wrote of the event:

"Pershing approached, he walked with perfect West Point precision, but his eyes saw everything, including a very young Lieutenant and his platoon. Pershing paused, the Lieutenant saluted smartly, Pershing returned the salute with equal smartness.

"Of course it was silly of the Lieutenant to think for an instant that General Pershing would bother to inspect one little platoon, one trifling handful, when he had come to inspect the entire division. Yet Pershing was there in front of him, he had come only to inspect, he did not expect the Lieutenant to make a speech and the Lieutenant knew that Pershing was not going to make a speech. There was but one thing to do, absurd as it seemed to him, form his little handful of men for inspection.

" 'Open ranks— March!'

"The Lieutenant gave the command, the doughboys whipped into formation for inspection as if they were automatons with brand new and extra snappy springs inside them instead of human muscles.

"Pershing's face was about as expressive as that of the Sphinx. He walked down between the short lines, the boys, who only yesterday had been sent over from Plattsburg, following and, so far as he can now remember, quite forgetting to breathe.

"Brigadier Generals and Colonels and Lieutenant Colonels and Majors of the division waited, and waited. Pershing looked at every man in the platoon, at every button, legging, gun—there wasn't a detail that his sharp eyes missed. Suddenly he stopped in front of a Corporal and looked at him sharply, looked him straight in the eye.

"The Corporal stared straight ahead, not at Pershing but through him. He was as motionless as a pyramid, he didn't bat an eyelash. Pershing was so pleased that he almost permitted himself to smile."

By mid-July, the A.E.F. occupied Château-Thierry and compelled Hindenburg himself to write grudgingly that the Americans had "proved themselves clumsily but firmly led. They had taken our weak units by supreme surprise thanks to their numerical superiority."

Upwards of 200,000 United States troops were fighting that month along the broad Aisne-Marne front. It was the largest military effort thus far in the history of their nation.

Victory, however, was never won without cost, and the European war was proving this once again. As Henry Russell Miller, with the First Division, wrote:

"During the third day before Soissons, there was a tiny knoll that, they told me, was taken and retaken six times, at the end remaining in our lines. Toward nightfall there was a lull in the storm; one could go forward with comparative safety. Just at dusk I came to the slope leading up that knoll. And everywhere I looked the trampled wheat was dotted by recumbent figures. There was one field, two or three acres, on which it seemed you could not have stood ten feet from some one of those figures. They might have been wearied troops that had thrown themselves down to sleep. They slept indeed, the sleep no earthly reveille could disturb. . . ."

(*Left*) **Brigadier General Benjamin Foulois, an aerial scout in the Villa chase, arrives at Issoudon to become the A.E.F.'s aviation chief.** NATIONAL ARCHIVES (*Right*) **A tough old campaigner of Samoa, Cuba, the Philippines and Vera Cruz, Brigadier General John A. Lejeune quickly distinguished himself in France.** U. S. MARINE CORPS

Pershing, these hot days of July, divided his time between head-quarters and the front. He traveled either in his command limousine, a 30-horsepower Dodge named Daisy, at breakneck speed, or in a well-equipped railway car under the personal housekeeping of the former manager of the LaSalle Hotel, in Chicago.

On July 20, the Commander-in-Chief inspected the sector held by Brigadier General Thomas W. Darrah, of the 55th Brigade, 28th Division. He was not pleased with what he found.

It seemed to the Commander-in-Chief that the brigade's right had been left "in the air"—unprotected on account of the sudden withdrawal of the French 125th Division. Darrah was peremptorily ordered by Pershing never again to turn his men over to French command without first "satisfying himself as to all orders in the case."

The town where he spoke to Darrah, and also General Dickman, of

A trusted aide was Colonel George C. Marshall. NATIONAL ARCHIVES

the 3rd Division, Courboin, was "particularly dirty and badly shot up."
It was in command of Major Peck of the Dental Corps who "admitted it
was dirty but claimed he had no men to clean it up." Pershing continued:

". . . Thence went to La Ferté-sous-Jouarre, headquarters 1st.
Corps. Had luncheon with General Liggett. Learned that the attack on
front between Château-Thierry to Soissons was to be resumed at 3
o'clock. Went to General Edwards' headquarters [26th Division] in the
outskirts of Méry-sur-Marne. Went over with him his plan for attack, and
left for headquarters of the 3d corps [General Bullard] which I had been
told was at Montgorbet, northeast of Villers-Cotterets.

"While at General Edwards' headquarters a 'phone message came
from General Pétain asking if I could not come to his headquarters to
dinner to talk over urgent matters with him. I accepted. In the forest of
Villers-Cotterets I met General Mangin who was, like myself, making
slow headway in the jam of artillery, wagons, trucks, ambulances with
wounded, and detachments of troops which were all going or coming
along that badly cut-up route. General Mangin told me I would not find
headquarters at Montgorbet, but rather at Taillefontaine. Anyway I went

on there and found by chance Lieutenant Colonel Clark, of the G-3 Corps, who was passing through with orders for the First Division.

"I followed his car northward to Couevres, over a country which had all the marks of recent battle. In a quarry to the west of the town the First Division headquarters was working in a large room about 300 x 200 feet dug into the side of a hill.

"I talked with Colonel King, congratulated him and the division commander through him, had dinner there under ground and left for Taillefontaine. Passed the train of the British divisions which were coming to take positions south of Soissons.

". . . The time in the meantime had been passing. It was after 8 o'clock when we left. I had fortunately had a 'phone message sent to General Pétain that I would not be there till about 10:30. The road was bad, long and crowded. Darkness came on with wind and rain, and with delays incident to looking at signboards and maps to be sure of the way, we arrived at Provins at 1:30 in the night.

"Arrangements had been made to put us up at Major Clark's house, and we lost no time getting to bed."

Then he was off for Bordeaux, accompanied by Colonel Andrews, now his assistant chief of staff, who wrote:

"At Bordeaux, General Pershing made an informal speech to a large number of enlisted men working on the docks, including many colored stevedores. Enlisted men, as well as many other people, generally have a grievance which they enjoy talking about, and many of these men thought they wanted to serve at the front. Their work was hard, but it was more important to the A.E.F. than they could possibly know or appreciate. Standing on a pile of lumber, General Pershing talked to them in a plain but forceful manner, emphasizing the important and patriotic character of their work which he said was equal to that of any other man in France, expressing his personal interest in and appreciation of all they had accomplished, and urging them to still greater effort in the future. . . .

"Before commencing his talk General Pershing told his aide, Boyd, to circulate quietly among the men and observe their reaction to his talk. Boyd came back with a story about a colored stevedore who asked him what the General meant by saying he would send some of them to the front. Boyd explained, to which the colored stevedore replied,

" 'Well, boss, I'se now about as close to dem front line trenches as I cares to be.' "

A few days later, back in Chaumont, Pershing was entertaining King George V.

"As per program," Pershing methodically reported, "the King of England arrived at 11:15 and presented to me, in the Château, the decoration of the Grand Cross of the Order of the Bath and to General Bliss the Order of Saint Michael and Saint George. As the King, General Bliss and I were in a room alone, the King took advantage of this opportunity to talk to me about the employment of American troops.

"He is very anxious to have as many of them as possible serve with the British Army, and stated that their presence had a tremendous effect in backing up the morale of the British and the French; that the British had never lost spirit, but that after the March drive they were very sorely tired. He stated that he was not a politician and did not see from that point of view, but he thought it very advantageous to have some Americans with the troops serving with the British. He stated that Dunkirk could be placed at our disposition as a port. He indulged in some sentiments as to how much it would mean after the war to say that the two English-speaking races fought side by side in this struggle, and again mentioned the confidence which would be inspired by the presence of American troops with the British.

"I should have liked to argue with the King and set him right on a good many matters in this connection, but seeing that he is a King and that what he thinks will have very little influence on the situation anyway, I let it go by informing him politely that it is not intended to have the Americans serve either with the French or with the British, but that we are now forming armies of our own for which we have sufficient troops."

Later the same day, Pershing met with General Haig in the latter's private railway car near Wiry-aux-Bois. The Commander-in-Chief was still raging inwardly at a letter Haig had written concerning the use of several American divisions in a forthcoming British offensive.

"I informed him of my own plans and told him that I should like to withdraw from the British front three of my five divisions which are now serving there. The conversation was not pleasant for awhile, though we both kept quite within the bounds of politeness. I reminded him of the projects discussed with Marshal Foch at our last meeting at his place, and also made it very clear to him that I propose to form an American Army and did not propose to have my troops used here, there and the other place at the will of any allies. He remarked rather gingerly in the course of the conversation that these divisions were sent up there to fight and that now I propose to withdraw them without their having participated in any battle. . . .

"I told Marshal Haig that I had not come to his headquarters to bring out a discussion of withdrawing my troops at the moment when he was in a battle, and that I had no intention of leaving him in an embarrassing position. He confessed to seeing my point of view and agreed to the withdrawal of the divisions."

Pershing was still fighting for the integrity of the A.E.F. with Foch, as well as with Haig. In a heated conference he declared:

"Marshal Foch, you have no authority as Allied Commander-in-Chief to call upon me to yield up my command of the American Army and have it scattered among the Allied forces where it will not be an American Army at all. . . . You may insist all you please, but I decline absolutely to agree to your plan. While our Army will fight wherever you may decide, it will not fight except as an independent American Army."

And "Black Jack" meant just that.

10

Autumn in the Argonne

THOSE who could not be—or preferred not to be—in France the summer of 1918 found vicarious excitement at the motion pictures, and especially at theaters where the film *Why America Will Win* was showing. Purportedly the life story of General Pershing, the picture wove into a modest amount of footage of newsreels a plethora of pure Hollywood fabrication. The smashing climax depicted Pershing's singlehanded capture of the Kaiser and the Crown Prince, both of whom treacherously attempted to murder the American general. Pershing was forced to shoot the Crown Prince, though, providentially, a lightning bolt stayed the Kaiser's killer's hand.

In France, the Commander-in-Chief in late August and early September was planning on a capture, but the object was neither Kaiser Wilhelm nor his son. It was the once pretty village of St. Mihiel and the outjutting salient it commanded—the primary object of Pershing's military plans ever since he had arrived in France.

It would be, this time, an American operation by an American Army (with French support). Created for this specific purpose was the First Army, comprised of half a million troops. Its principal general was none other than John J. Pershing. However, he entrusted heavy responsibilities to three hand-picked corps commanders, Major Generals Hunter Liggett, Joseph T. Dickman, and George H. Cameron.

111

In the late summer and fall, 1918, eastern France was ravaged anew as the Kaiser's armies drew back. This spectacularly clear photograph shows Thiaucourt under German fire. NATIONAL ARCHIVES

While the Army was being assembled—both men and matériel—G-2 became concerned over the extent of espionage all along the front lines. It was well known among the Germans that the Americans were planning to smash into St. Mihiel.

How, under such compromising conditions, could the offensive go forward with a degree of surprise?

The Commander-in-Chief himself devised the answer: deceive the enemy by elaborate employment of counterintelligence. He wrote orders "establishing" First Army headquarters in Belfort, an historic town on the Swiss border, but nearly 100 miles south of St. Mihiel.

Pershing went further. He sent a complete headquarters staff to Belfort. Commanded by a full colonel, who alone was "let in" on the large-scale deception, the staffers went about renting buildings and actually moving desks and file cabinets into offices. Mail couriers commenced a regular thrice-daily service into the city on their motorcycles —noisy attention-attracters in themselves—and over the newly rented inn a large sign, emblazoned with the American flag, was hammered into place: HEADQUARTERS.

Nestling next to a neutral country, Belfort could safely be considered a nest of international cloak-and-daggery and all the attendant intrigue. Just to be sure that the word would be carried back to Germany, the colonel left a copy of his orders, stamped SECRET in big black letters, setting up the First Army "headquarters," on the bed of his hotel room.

When he returned, the "orders"—just as he had expected—were gone.

By the first week in September, time was nearing for the great offensive. Pershing issued terse, understandable orders:

The First Army will reduce the St. Mihiel salient.

It did.

Pershing, who stood next to Secretary of War Baker, just arrived in France, on the heights of the Meuse, reported the battle in these succinct terms:

The 108th Field Artillery firing at the retreating Germans at the start of the vast Meuse-Argonne offensive. NATIONAL ARCHIVES

"After four hours artillery preparation, the seven American divisions in the front line advanced at 5 A.M. on September 12, assisted by a limited number of tanks manned partly by Americans and partly by the French. These divisions, accompanied by groups of wire cutters and others armed with Bangalore torpedoes, went through the successive bands of barbed wire that protected the enemy's front line and support trenches in irresistible waves on schedule time, breaking down all defense of an enemy demoralized by the great volume of our artillery fire and our sudden approach out of the fog. . . .

"At the cost of only 7,000 casualties, mostly light, we had taken 16,000 prisoners and 443 guns, a great quantity of material, released the inhabitants of the many villages from enemy domination, and established our lines in a position to threaten Metz."

It was learned that three German divisions actually had been removed from the salient to guard against the mythical offensive at Belfort.

No one to hold a grudge, Foch, who had opposed Pershing's independent action, wired the A.E.F.'s commander a message of congratulations upon his "magnificent victory by a maneuver skillfully prepared as well as valiantly executed."

Woodrow Wilson himself cabled that "the boys have done what we expected of them."

The St. Mihiel offensive had been planned as the last major American effort of 1918. The big push was expected after a winter of recuperation and further organization.

But Pershing changed his mind. He felt, as Foch did, that the German Army was badly disorganized, the Allies had the initiative, and it was the time to strike. Just as the A.E.F. was poised at the St. Mihiel salient, certain officers were suddenly and secretly transferred from the operation to start planning for "Our Greatest Battle."

The Americans were to launch an attack in an area where there had been a stalemate from the Argonne to the Swiss border since the beginning of the war. It presented the greatest natural obstacles on the whole front, with the Vosges mountains and the adjoining Alps forming a mighty barricade.

The new offensive was to be between the Meuse River and the western edge of the Argonne Forest. The terrain there, too, was perfect for the defense; a series of shelving ridges, one after another leading from higher to still higher ground.

But Pershing felt his men were equal to the task and he saw victory

A lonely observation post at Montfaucon. NATIONAL ARCHIVES

"We made steady headway in the almost impenetrable and strongly held Argonne Forest. . . ." U. S. ARMY PHOTOGRAPH

"Our dogged offensive was wearing down the enemy. . . ." U. S. ARMY PHOTOGRAPH

Trenches in '65 and '17: a contrast between doughboys in France

in sight, even as Grant had in the final weeks before Richmond, or Sherman on his march through Georgia. He set up field headquarters in the town hall of Souilly, on the road from Bar-le-Duc to Verdun. The offices, in fact, had formerly been occupied by Marshal Pétain, when he directed the defense of Verdun with the rallying cry, "They shall not pass!"

"Our advance," Pershing wrote, "is somewhat checked by rather persistent action of Germans with machine guns. This is due to a certain extent to the lack of experience and lack of push on the part of division and brigade commanders. Montfaucon was not taken yesterday [September 26] and the 79th Division remained still in front of it this morning. About noon I gave energetic instructions that it should be taken by one means or another. The 4th Division was beyond and to the right of Montfaucon. Gave them instructions to move toward the west.

"In the afternoon the 79th Division proceeded to the capture of the town. The 77th Division withstood a counter-attack in the Argonne Forest. The 28th Division made fair progress only and the 35th Division did not progress satisfactorily.

"General Robert H. Noble of the 79th Division was relieved from

and Grant's army before Petersburg. U. S. ARMY PHOTOGRAPH

command by his division commander. General Frederick S. Foltz was also relieved by his division commander.

"The 4th Division has done very well, also the 80th. The 33rd has made satisfactory progress. On the whole I am not very much pleased with the progress made, though it should not be called unsatisfactory."

The next day the Commander-in-Chief visited the front in person and did "all in my power to instill an aggressive spirit in the different corps commanders."

The continuing, grinding action that ensued came to be known as the Meuse-Argonne offensive. A strong point before the so-called Kriemhilde Line, the Argonne Forest commanded the counterinvasion route to the fortress city and major rail center, Metz; in fact, to all of Lorraine and, ultimately, the Rhine River.

On into October the steady advance of the A.E.F. continued, as more and more conquered territory was liberated and German prisoners taken in increasing, revealing numbers.

"In the chill rain of dark nights," Pershing wrote, "our engineers had to build new roads across spongy, shell-torn areas, repair broken roads beyond No Man's Land, and build bridges. Our gunners, with no

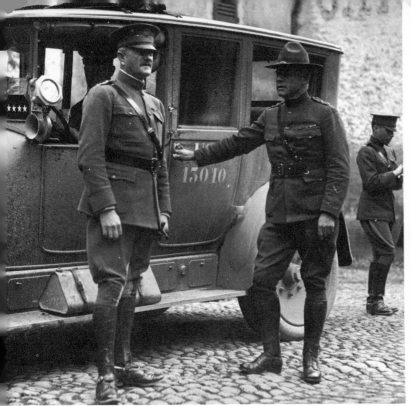

(Left) **Pershing with his classmate Major General Charles T. Menoher, Commanding the VI Corps, at Essey.** *(Right)* **Pause in the fighting long enough to decorate a brave officer: Brigadier General Douglas MacArthur.** NATIONAL ARCHIVES

thought of sleep, put their shoulders to wheels and dragropes to bring their guns through the mire in support of the infantry, now under the increasing fire of the enemy's artillery."

In the face of fresh German divisions desperately hurled into battle in an effort to stem the American tide, the advance continued:

"We made steady headway in the almost impenetrable and strongly held Argonne Forest for, despite this reinforcement, it was our Army that was doing the driving. Our aircraft was increasing in skill and numbers and forcing the issue, and our infantry and artillery were improving rapidly with each new experience. . . .

"Our day by day pressure against the enemy brought day by day more prisoners, mostly survivors from machine gun nests captured in fighting at close quarters. . . .

"Our dogged offensive was wearing down the enemy, who continued desperately to throw his best troops against us, thus weakening his line in front of our Allies and making their advance less difficult."

Edwin L. James, *New York Times* correspondent, started his story on one day's action:

In the cold rain of the clammy mid-October of northern France the doughboys of the American Army again today hit the first German line north of Verdun. Against a concentration of machine guns never before equalled, placed in natural position of great strategic advantage, Pershing's men drove their wedge deeper into the Kriemhilde Line. . . .

Secretary Baker wrote to President Wilson at this time, outlining in detail the obstacles, both personal and military, confronting General Pershing:

". . . a noteworthy instance of his [General Sir Henry Wilson's] unreliability occurred just before the St. Mihiel drive, when the plan for that movement was shown him. He protested so fiercely to Lord Milner [Britain's new Secretary of State for War] against its being undertaken that Lord Milner actually adopted his opinion and committed it to writing against the movement, and was deeply humiliated and chagrined at our success at St. Mihiel which showed him the extent to which he had been beguiled by Sir Henry Wilson.

"Before the St. Mihiel action Sir Henry Wilson said openly in England with regard to it that one or the other of two things would take place. Either we would find less resistance than we expected, in which case our staff would be unable to manage our troops and they would

The last photo of Quentin Roosevelt, and his grave. He died in an air duel on July 14 near Chamery, 10 kilometers north of the Marne River.

Even during the largest, most decisive battles, inspections must continue. Pershing paused at this town near the front long enough to look into Marine billets. NATIONAL ARCHIVES

Pickets even in the front lines never knew who would pop up at their posts next. Here, Samuel Gompers, the labor leader, shakes a doughboy's hand. NATIONAL ARCHIVES

rush beyond their objective and be trapped; or else we would find more resistance than we expected and get nowhere, with great losses of men and material. The event completely disappointed his predictions. The staff management of that action was admirable, and its success complete, with more than three times as many prisoners as our entire casualty list, including the slightly wounded.

"You may be interested to know too why the progress on General Pershing's front in this general battle is slow. The front from the Meuse to the Argonne Forest, on which General Pershing's attack is being made, is probably as difficult ground as there is anywhere on the entire Western Front, and certainly more difficult than any place where active battles are now being waged. In addition to that, the attack threatens Mezières, which is the great railroad center on the Sedan-Metz line. Should Mezières fall, the German communications for supplies would be completely cut and the withdrawal of all their forces to the west would have to be by insufficient and round-about railroads through Namur and other points far to the north. It is the one place on the line where the Germans cannot afford either to withdraw or retire, and as a consequence the heaviest enemy concentration anywhere on the line is directly ahead of General Pershing. . . ."

One afternoon, as the fighting continued in the Meuse-Argonne, like the fire and rumble of an unending summer thunderstorm, Lejeune, now a major general, commanding the battle-wise Second Division, was driving along a shattered country road. It led to the pin-point village, Les Ilettes.

Suddenly there was a roar, and "two big limousines going at the rate of about 70 miles an hour" passed.

"In the leading car," reported General Lejeune, "we caught a glimpse of General Pershing. He always travelled at full speed and was followed by an emergency car for his use in case anything should happen to the car in which he was riding. The thought of the heavy burden which he carried by night and by day saddened me. It was a burden which he could never lay aside.

"He had no periods of rest behind the lines such as we have been experiencing. The successful prosecution of the task allotted to his armies, and the honor as well as the security of our country were always in his thoughts, and on his decisions there depended the life or death of thousands of men as well as victory or defeat for our arms."

Pershing's aide, Colonel John G. Quekemeyer, could attest to this

Throwing hand grenades at the enemy (probably the Austrians) on the Piave. NATIONAL ARCHIVES

A 14-inch railway gun firing in the Argonne Forest. NATIONAL ARCHIVES

(Left) The village is Exermont. Two doughboys are running for their lives down a street under mortar bombardment. A German lies dead in the road, showing the proximity of the enemy. Behind is a disabled Allied tank. The two soldiers may have been the tank crew. NATIONAL AR-CHIVES

Members of the 18th Infantry, First Division, crouching in shell holes on Hill 240 in the Ardennes. NATIONAL AR-CHIVES

very burden within his commanding officer's heart. One evening, as they drove through the chill dark, Pershing suddenly put his hands to his face and muttered: "My God, I sometimes wonder how I can go on."

The war was waste. The war was unfairness and cruelty. There was soul-sadness in many hearts besides that of the Commander-in-Chief. His daily mail attested, in compounding volume, to this tragedy which had come to dwell in great and lowly places.

One such letter out of the mounting heap was addressed to General Pershing personally—"dear friend"—from Adeline Tinkey, of Clayton, Iowa:

> *Just a line to you. I have been trying to find my son since May the 15th. His name, Samuel B. Tinkey, Co. E, 132 Infantry. He left Texas about May 11th as far as I can make out for he wrote to me from Camp Upton, Long Island, New York, May the 13th, that is, he dated his letter and he said he could give me no address and I got his letter May the 15th and I have been writing ever since. I am almost frantic with grief. If I knew he was dead then I would try to reconcile myself the best I could. He is our only child and was our only support. We are both old and got nothing too good but if my son is under your command I would thank you as no mother could thank you any more. Hoping to hear from you soon. I remain,*
>
> *Your obedient servant*

Major General George Bell, Jr., Commanding the 33rd Division, replied:

> *The Commanding General of the American Expeditionary Forces, General John J. Pershing, has directed me to send you an answer.*
>
> *I give you with earnest regret the information that your son, Samuel B. Tinkey, Co. E, 132d Infantry, died in France in Casualty Clearing Station No. 41 on the 9th day of August, from the effects of being gassed by the enemy while on the field of battle.*
>
> *My sincere sympathy goes to you in this loss but I know that you will bear the grief as befits the brave mother of a brave son. . . .*

The Great War continued.

The supply train moves up on a foggy morning in the Argonne.
NATIONAL ARCHIVES

11

A "Great Adventure" Ends

THE Kaiser's armies had been crushed on all fronts. They were retreating, though with surprising discipline, toward the Homeland. Bulgaria and Turkey were out of the war. Ludendorff resigned to avoid formal dismissal. In Kiel, the German Navy was mutinying.

What had seemed impossible in the summer of 1914 was happening: the disintegration of the German fighting machine.

Marshal von Hindenburg attributed the Central Powers' final defeat to the massive push which Pershing had led throughout October.

"The pressure," the German commander wrote, "which the fresh American masses were putting upon our most sensitive point in the region of the Meuse was too strong."

General Pershing himself, though suffering from a mild attack of the Spanish influenza which was ravaging most of the world, was immensely preoccupied as his armies pushed farther and farther east, menacing two great objectives: Metz and Sedan. The Commander-in-Chief of the A.E.F. nonetheless continued to maintain immense personal equanimity and measured judgment, attributing such qualities, in part, to his habit of "dismissing a subject from my mind, once it was settled."

Considering his great responsibilities and considering the vast numbers of men he was leading into the mortal perils of war far from their homes, criticism leveled at him was not disproportionate.

There was one story, perhaps unkind, but not necessarily apocryphal, purporting to paraphrase the conversation of two doughboys.

"Pershing," one observed dourly, "says he will take Metz if it costs a hundred thousand lives."

His buddy plodded along in silence for a few moments, then replied, "Ain't he a darned generous guy!"

An undercurrent of grumbling did arise by October, sparked in measure by Pershing's overwhelming faith in the rifle. Even at St. Mihiel, the German machine gunners, together with the German artillery, had reaffirmed what the British had been taught in 1914—the infantryman and his rifle had a place but not the same place as at Gettysburg, or San Juan Hill.

In these dying days of the war, the question was not merely surrender, but—the terms of surrender. Colonel Edward M. House, President Wilson's special adviser, was in France meeting with the Allies on these very questions. He was a man whom Pershing found personally distasteful, and whom he refused even to address as "Colonel," since the title was honorary, rather than military.

On October 30, the Commander-in-Chief of the A.E.F. was in Paris conferring with House.

"On meeting Mr. House," Pershing wrote, "at the Foreign Office, I gave him a copy of a paper I had been considering for some time. The paper set forth the question as to whether we should grant an armistice to Germany at this time. I took the position that it should not be granted. In the evening I received a note from Mr. House asking me what were the views of the other military commanders on this question. I sent Boyd to tell him that I did not know the opinion of the others, that I had never discussed the matter with them.

"Mr. House asked Boyd what my idea was in submitting this paper. He told Boyd that the question as to whether or not an armistice should be granted was purely political and that all the prime ministers were anxious for it. Boyd told him that I had not expressed my reasons for presenting the paper but that my point of view was naturally a military one. He said he had shown it to Lloyd George and M. Clemenceau, who did not seem to consider it.

"I wrote him a note telling him that my consideration was, of course, only military."

There was nothing equivocal about Pershing's stand. He told House, simply, the Allies should demand "unconditional surrender."

Major General Tasker H. Bliss, A.E.F. Chief of Staff, and Pershing meet in front of the Hôtel Crillon, Paris. NATIONAL ARCHIVES

The events moved swiftly. Some kind of surrender obviously was no more than days distant. On November 8, in his railroad car parked at Souilly, Pershing received a telephone message from Foch stating that hostilities would definitely cease upon a day and time to be fixed later.

"I decided," Pershing wrote, "to go to Paris to get in closer touch with the Marshal in order to talk over either the prospected operation or the part we are to play in occupying German or Alsatian territory. I gave up an engagement to meet a Japanese mission at 2:30 and left immediately after luncheon by motor for Paris, arriving at about 7:30 P.M."

There he saw Colonel T. Bentley Mott, a West Point classmate, who advised that "the German plenipotentiaries had met Marshal Foch at Guise at 9 A.M. and had found the terms a little harder than expected and consequently had sent a message back by automobile to Spa at about 11 A.M. If the Germans answer by wireless we may hear tonight. If they send a messenger back the earliest hour we could hear would be about noon tomorrow.

"I find that Mott had been given the message he sent with the understanding that he should hold it until he got word that the Armistice was signed and that he should send it immediately on notification that the Armistice was signed."

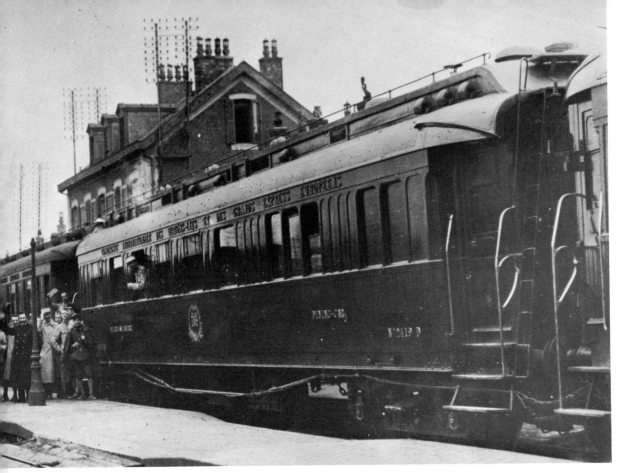

The surrender car, Wagons-Lits No. 2419D, at Compiègne, November 11. NATIONAL ARCHIVES

The Commander-in-Chief of the A.E.F. was in Chaumont on November 11 when he was given the word. He wrote:

"Telephonic message from Colonel Mott received at 6 A.M. informing me that the Armistice had been signed and that hostilities would cease at 11 o'clock on the 11th. This order was immediately transmitted to the armies by telephone. It seems that both the First and Second armies had planned attacks for this morning. I have begun studying the questions that are brought up by this new condition.

"Had a talk with General Nolan about organizing a more important bureau for handling visitors."

The rest of his day was spent at Chaumont, although he planned to leave for Paris that night by train.

Thus, Pershing's own observance of the hour of 11 A.M., so long awaited and prayed for by the world, was in the nature of anticlimax. The end of the Great War was attended by much more emotion and demonstration elsewhere.

In newly liberated cities and towns the soldiers' paths were strewn with garlands. At Mons, the British and Canadian troops were on hand to receive the accolades.

Paris went almost unrestrainedly wild, with the Place de la Concorde a hub of celebration. American soldiers, wherever they appeared in the streets, were grabbed by Frenchwomen and kissed and kissed again until their cheeks were sore.

In Berlin, the contrasts were stark. Revolutionaries fed the flames of chaos and civil insurrection all day. The Kaiser was in Holland. Nonetheless, his horses, to the Reds, were themselves symbols of loathing. With machine guns they riddled the royal stables at Schlosshof.

In London, where it was a misty, chilly Monday, Prime Minister Lloyd George arose in the House of Commons and announced in a choked voice, "This is no time for words . . ."

The King and Queen appeared on a balcony at Buckingham Palace to acknowledge the cheers of their assembled subjects, while the Irish Guards band serenaded them with "Rule Britannia!"

French poilus waving at No. 2419D at the Compiegne station.
NATIONAL ARCHIVES

A lorry lumbered along the Strand, filled with soldiers who were firing blanks from their rifles. Thinking it an air raid, passers-by scrambled for doorways and cellars. It was well past 11 o'clock before it occurred to the disciplined, phlegmatic citizens of London that the war was really over.

"It was mainly an organized though orderly spectacle of movement," noted Edgar B. Pier, of the Portland *Oregonian*, "without any great variety of stunts or picturesque incidents. Perhaps the crowd did not know how to do things as they do in America; or perhaps it was merely content to go and go—and then come back."

At Trafalgar, exceptions to the day's rule of restraint snatched signboards off passing omnibuses and built a huge bonfire.

Across the Atlantic, the first news flashes had arrived at 3 A.M. By dawn, factory whistles were shrieking and church bells were ringing from Savannah to San Francisco. In a few communities, such as Newport News, Virginia, there was wanton damage to property. In most cities there were parades, endless parades, cheering, shouting, flag waving, and lionizing of anyone found wearing a uniform.

All of a sudden the guns grew quiet and it was safe to stand upright in a trench once more. NATIONAL ARCHIVES

11 A.M. **November 11, somewhere in the American sector.** NATIONAL
ARCHIVES

On November 12, Pershing, still not celebration-minded, arrived in
Paris, then continued on to Senlis to meet Foch whom he found "in high
spirits and said a great many things about the splendid work of the
American Army, my cordial cooperation and how he appreciated my
straight-forward dealing. He said that he had always known my attitude
on every question because I stated it frankly and clearly and then lived
up to it. He became so enthusiastic and so did I that both of us were
unable to restrain the tears, and the Marshal in his enthusiasm gave me
an old-fashioned French 'accolade.'

"The object of my visit was to decorate him with the Distinguished
Service Medal. Behind his headquarters he had lined up a guard, apparently of territorial orderlies, about 17 in number, under command of
a sergeant. The trumpeters furnished the music. The Marshal faced the
command. I stood between him and them and made a very short speech

in French, the tenor of which is given in a letter which was signed by me and handed by Boyd to one of the Marshal's aides. I then pinned the medal on him and shook hands with him. The Marshal made quite a long talk, stating how much he appreciated the honor and how brilliantly the Americans had acted. He seemed very much impressed. He then shook hands with me very cordially and stood holding my hand with both of his as he ordered the trumpeters to close the 'ban.' "

At lunch General Weygand told Pershing about the arrival of the German emissaries.

"It seems that they came across the line by automobile on the afternoon of November 7 and got into a special car or train which was sent to meet them by the French. This car was moved during the night to a point in the forest between Compiègne and Soissons on an A.L.P.G. siding. The train of the Marshal had been moved to a siding alongside of the track of the German train during the night. A kind of ramp joined the two trains.

"The Emissaries were ushered into the Marshal's train and the Marshal asked to whom he had the honor to speak. They told them who they were and he asked them if they had credentials. Ertzberger took out from his pocket a soiled envelope which contained the credentials of the party signed by Max de Bade.

"The Marshal took these credentials out of the room and examined them, and returning asked them what was the object of their visit. They replied that they had come to discuss terms of armistice. Marshal Foch made it clear that he himself was not asking for an armistice and did not care to have one. He then asked the Germans if they wished an armistice.

"They said that they did. The Marshal said if they wished an armistice, here were the terms upon which they might have it, and handed them the terms. General Weygand said that the members were apparently very much depressed by the severity of the terms. They had no power to sign the armistice without consent of the chancellor, and after some little discussion they sent an officer, Capt. Heldorff, with the armistice terms across the lines to the German side. During the 9th and 10th, while waiting for directions from the German government, the Germans talked very freely with General Weygand about conditions in Germany and spoke particularly about the lack of food and the fear there would be famine because of the bad transportation service.

"In the armistice terms they did not seem to object to turning over 5,000 cannon, but deplored the condition which required that 30,000

Grateful doughboys tack up a sign in Paris to honor their President. U. S. ARMY PHOTOGRAPH

It's all over, over there. Doughboys wait at a snowy railroad station near Château-Villain. NATIONAL ARCHIVES

Paris celebrates the Armistice. NATIONAL ARCHIVES

The Commander-in-Chief personally led the victory parade past the Arc de Triomphe. NATIONAL ARCHIVES

machine guns be turned over. They finally succeeded in obtaining from the Marshal a reduction to 25,000 machine guns so that they might have some for riot duty. They complained about the short time allowed them for evacuation, stating that the German army was in no condition to move, either forward or backward.

"The delegates were apparently very much impressed with the fairmindedness of General Weygand, and on the 10th they drew up a number of requests which they wished to make to Marshal Foch. They handed this paper first to General Weygand, asking him to go over it, and let them know if there were any requests contained in it which General Weygand thought would not be accorded by the Marshal.

"Naturally, General Weygand turned the paper over to the Marshal. In speaking of the danger of riots in Germany, the delegates were asked why they did not send more of their reserve divisions to maintain order in the interior of their country. Their reply was that they had no divisions in reserve; that every division that they had was actually in line.

"A wireless message from the German government authorizing the delegates to sign the armistice was received about 11 P.M. on the 10th.

It took until about 2 A.M. on the 11th to decode the message, and discussion with the Marshal began immediately. It took until about 5 A.M. to complete the discussion and draw up the terms in the rough.

"In their hurry to stop bloodshed, the last page of the conditions was written first, on which the signatures were placed at 5 minutes after 5 A.M. on the 11th and word was sent out immediately to the troops to stop hostilities at 11 A.M. The other pages were written afterward.

"General Weygand said that the delegates left soon after. Just before they left, Mr. Oberndorff stated that he would like to speak to General Weygand. General Weygand and he walked up and down in the woods by the train for a few minutes. The German stated that he wished to thank the General for all his courtesy during the negotiations; also, he wished to ask General Weygand if it would not be possible to have started in France in some of the French newspapers a little propaganda in favor of sending food to the German population. He called attention to the fact that no one wanted to let the German people starve and that it was not to the interest of France to let them do so."

Weygand then coldly said his courtesy was simply "a matter of duty" and that the Germans evidently had no idea of the "deepest

It was quite embarrassing, belatedly acknowledging a salute—
Thanksgiving Day, 1918 at Chaumont. (*Right*) After the Armistice,
his son, Warren, came over to join him. NATIONAL ARCHIVES

These officers came to Chaumont to be decorated.

rooted hatred" in France for what the Germans had done to them and their country. He added that any French paper which published such "propaganda . . . would rightly be burned." Somewhat abashed, the Germans forecast to Weygand that someday the French would "understand."

Weygand managed to have the final word. If he and the German emissaries ever met again, he assured them, "it would probably be in Heaven."

There remained now but the problems of occupation, demobilization and moving the 2 million troops of the A.E.F. home. The German people themselves helped to make the former concern a more simple one than had been envisioned. Lieutenant Colonel Paul H. Clark, of the Quartermaster Corps, transportation branch, wrote Pershing from Bitburg, Germany, of the local attitude toward the occupying forces.

"The people line the streets as we pass, they are seemingly undemonstrative, rather indifferent, it would seem, but the longer we remain in a given place there appears to be an increase of good will by the people. There are individuals who cry 'Vive la France' as we march along the streets.

General Pétain receiving the baton of a Marshal of France at Metz, December 8. Left to right, Joffre, Foch, Haig (behind Haig, Weygand), Pershing, Gillain (Belgium), Albricci (Italy) and Haller (Poland). NATIONAL ARCHIVES

"The attitude of the Germans toward the French Army of occupation is another indication of the difference between the characters of the two people. When the Germans marched into Paris in the war of 1870 not a soul was on the streets, not even a cat, everyone, every animal even, was indoors and the shutters of every window were closed. The intensity of feeling was great. But the Boche are in striking contrast. They seem to feel little repugnance to lining the streets as we march past and occasionally some individual yells 'Vive la France!' And they seem to feel less and less, the longer we stay, any feeling of resentment.

"Now this difference is explained in some degree by the fact that the French have been a definite highly organized nation for centuries whereas Germany has been so divided politically, consequently the sentiments of nationality are much more deeply developed in Frenchmen than in Germans.

"It is very difficult to form a conclusion as to what the future of Germany is going to be. . . . I personally expect to see order reestablished in Germany inside of a few months."

Catching up with the news while recuperating. (*Right*) **Miss Good-win, of the YWCA, came to Chaumont to shake hands with the General.** NATIONAL ARCHIVES

Colonel Clark had referred largely to the arrival of French troops across the Rhine. The Bitburger *Zeitung* specifically wrote on December 7 of the Americans:

> *The occupation of the City and Circle by the American troops has been accomplished so far with no restriction of liberty or circulation. The officials and businessmen work in quiet and undisturbed. Life goes on as usual. The mails and railway traffic have necessarily been interrupted. It is just to acknowledge that the American Military authorities are efficient without harshness, and the behavior of the American troops is wonderfully good. Not only officers but soldiers are considerate and seem obliging. The Americans take pains not to make the occupation appear like vacations. . . .*

On Christmas Day, President Wilson, who had arrived for the peace talks, had dinner with Pershing at Chaumont. En route, the Chief Executive had inspected billets of the 103rd Infantry, Yankee (26th) Division. As Harry Benwell, one of the Division's members, reported the event:

"On each man's bunk was laid out his equipment, with each article in a certain place, as prescribed by regulations. Noticing a jointed stick, the President called it to the attention of General Pershing. The latter picked up the stick, and straightened it out, explained that it was one of the poles for a 'pup' tent, so-called—the little two-man tents which are carried on the march. After examining it, the President handed the pole back to General Pershing, who tossed it carelessly on to the bunk.

" 'But,' said President Wilson, 'suppose that man's bunk is inspected again? He would get into trouble with that pole lying like that. As your commanding officer I order you to replace the pole the way it should be!'

"General Pershing snapped to attention, saluted and replaced the pole in its proper position."

His face was red, as the rest of the official party chuckled. There weren't *many* men to whom Pershing had to accord the initial salute—aside from Congressional Medal of Honor winners, he could tick them off on the fingers of one hand. After all, he carried the same rank as Washington, Sherman, Grant and Sheridan.

He was not, however, a hero to or above criticism by all. In fact, he had made certain, unrelenting enemies, among them Major General

President Wilson came to Chaumont for Christmas dinner. NATIONAL ARCHIVES

Peyton C. March, Chief of Staff of the Army. He had fumed at his War Department offices in the anomalous position of exercising no real authority over Pershing or the A.E.F.

"General Pershing's inability," he wrote, "to function in teamwork with his legal and authorized superiors increased until it reached a point where he refused to obey Foch's orders abroad . . . he wanted a rubber stamp for Chief of Staff at home so he would be entirely independent of any supervisory control."

The war was over. The Allies, ostensibly, had won. The world was not interested one whit in the personal rivalries and animosities which had flared in the many general headquarters otherwise engaged for the most part in making that victory possible.

Winter settled once more over Lorraine, cold and white, a time for the quick, a time for the dead. While endless details of burial parties picked at the hard earth, others shivered in their billets and waited for those most desired of all orders—orders home.

Morale was at best fair; in some encampments, poor. The trouble was, as the newspapers from home already were attesting, everyone was

With spring, it was time to reap war's harvest. German prisoners help to landscape the American Cemetery, at Romagne, in the Argonne. NATIONAL ARCHIVES

It was time for the A.E.F. to start home. NATIONAL ARCHIVES

forgetting with unbelievable speed, the war and the A.E.F. as well.

Pershing, however, remained both busy and in good humor. On February 9, his friend General Bullard arrived in Chaumont from his own headquarters in Toul to receive a Belgian medal, the Order of Leopold.

"I stayed at General Pershing's house," Bullard penned in his diary. "The occasion was pleasant and profitable. General Pershing was in high spirits, joked and chatted. I felt quite stimulated as I always do when I meet bright men—men of consequence."

As winter turned into spring and spring into summer, 1919, the Commander-in-Chief occupied himself with the closing out of more and more A.E.F. components, as well as the writing of personal farewells to his friends and receiving similar letters—General Atterbury of the Pennsylvania Railroad, for example, wrote:

"Now that I am leaving I consider it fitting to express to you the keen admiration I feel for the brilliant success that has been attained by

The "great adventure" ends as Foch bids adieu to Pershing at Brest
on September 1, 1919. (*Right*) Someone told Pershing a very funny
joke, as he sailed for the United States aboard the "Leviathan."
NATIONAL ARCHIVES

the American Expeditionary Forces under your broad and intelligent
direction. With the passing of time and with the fuller study that will be
given the task that was committed to your charge in this war, its
stupendousness and the complexities entering into its handling will become more and more evident, and history cannot but allot most enviable
recognition to your leadership.

"It has been a genuine personal pleasure to me to serve under you
in the working out of your understanding. At all times you have manifested toward me in the relations that have brought us in contact, a
sympathetic and helpful feeling that always encouraged and inspired
the utmost effort."

Finally, on Monday the first of September, General Pershing's job
was finished. At Brest he clasped the hand of the man with whom he

had bitterly disputed so many momentous questions—Marshal Foch—and the two stood looking into each other's faces. Even the film in the many cameras that clicked on a close perimeter caught the telltale glisten in their eyes.

The generals then rode out together on the tender to the *Leviathan*, at anchor, smoke pouring from her three stacks. Though she was painted in drab gray, the wartime zigzag camouflage had now been removed.

Foch boarded the mighty liner for brief minutes, then, in the fashion of his country, quickly pressed his face to that of Pershing.

The French Marshal, and Supreme Allied Commander, walked down the gangplank to the waiting launch. Pershing remained as if frozen in a stiff salute.

Far forward, the anchor chains started their clank-clank-clank upward. The gulls screamed. The sun slanted over the red rooftops of the French port, shimmering in the later afternoon haze.

Foch gained the deck of the small craft, returned Pershing's salute. Slowly, almost mechanically, the latter allowed his hand to drop back toward his immaculately starched and pressed trousers.

The great adventure was over.

12

"As the Clock Strikes Noon . . ."

ON a sunny, warm morning, Monday, September 8, the *Leviathan* nosed into Pier 4, Hoboken, as thousands of people who had been up since dawn cheered.

"Oh, look!" exclaimed one of them, Mrs. Cecilia Farwell, of Carrollton, Missouri, thinking she had attracted the attention of General Pershing, from his lofty perch on the navigating bridge. "He took off his cap and gave me three bows!" It was a day of flutterings and many similar and simple elations.

President Wilson, in a note conveyed by Secretary Baker, asserted, "We are proud of you!"

The Commander-in-Chief of the A.E.F., briefly addressing his welcomers, extolled "those brave American men who fought for the undying principles of right and justice for mankind."

It was not an entirely happy nation to which the General returned. Boston's civic existence was colored and imperiled by a police strike. Soldiers were patrolling the streets and endeavoring to round up such known criminals, or even alleged criminals, as they could lay their untrained hands upon.

Wilson was in Seattle, on a national tour to plead for the League of Nations. Traveling a day or two behind him were such powerful senators as Hiram Johnson, Henry Cabot Lodge and Medill McCormick equally

147

Pershing is accorded a hero's welcome in Philadelphia. NATIONAL
ARCHIVES

determined to fragment the League into impotence, and seemingly nullify
much of what the A.E.F. had been sent to accomplish.

The country was gripped by local labor grievances and crimes such
as house breakings and purse snatchings. Race riots had flared in Knox-
ville.

Cost of living had soared everywhere, as Americans manifested
apprehension for the future, while strangely apathetic as to the moment.
Far too many doughboys had shed their uniforms, to find their old jobs
already filled. They had perhaps been heroes in 1917 and 1918—but this
was 1919.

Pershing was met with overwhelming ovations in New York and
Philadelphia. On September 17, astride his horse Kidron, he led a victory
parade down Pennsylvania Avenue, in Washington, and two days later
addressed a joint session of Congress.

Such functions became the pattern of his life that fall, a general
whose command was quickly reverting to one in name only. He had few
military duties in connection with the A.E.F. In December, he returned

After Philadelphia, that same September, the Commander-in-Chief leads a victory parade down Pennsylvania Avenue, in Washington. But the war, as one soldier, Henry Russell Miller, of the First Division, mused, was already forgotten by the vast majority of the populace: "Our fine fervor has vanished as the summer mist, souls have gone cold. The lonely, limping figure in khaki, still sometimes met on the street, we pass with careless glance. . . ." NATIONAL ARCHIVES

to Laclede. The Kansas City *Star* reported how his long-ago neighbors greeted him.

> He sat for a few minutes in his special car, the New York, smiling through the window, and waving his hand at old acquaintance after old acquaintance.
>
> "It is too much," he announced to Ed Allen, head of the welcome committee as Mayor of Laclede. "I'm going out and visit with them."
>
> The General had his way and the plans were hastily rearranged to permit the General to go to his old home, and then return to the depot to meet the Governor.
>
> A band from Brookfield struck up the tune of "When Johnnie

The Commander-in-Chief had earned a rest. The month after he returned home, Pershing went camping in New York State with friends. Included in the group (seated) is Colonel George C. Marshall. U. S. ARMY PHOTOGRAPH

Comes Marching Home." The tones were drowned out, as the General stepped to the door of his car, by the shouts of uncountable masses of humanity packing the surrounding vacant spaces to welcome the old Laclede boy.

Gazing over the crowd, General Pershing shouted to one after another, calling them by first names and nicknames of bygone days.

"Toad Welch!" and he pressed through the welcoming committee to grasp the outstretched hand of an elderly woman on the ground. Pulling on her arm and with her pushing with might and main, she was finally dragged through the press of eager people and jerked squarely into the arms of the General. He kissed her squarely on the lips and gave her a hug such as younger men would envy.

"Whom did you marry and where do you live?" he questioned in rapid fire.

"I'm now Mrs. L. W. Bosworth, and live in Kansas City, 2721 Wabash," she answered.

It was also time to catch up on duck hunting. PERSHING COLLECTION

. . . and horseback riding PERSHING COLLECTION

. . . and simple companionship with good friends like Charlie Dawes. PERSHING COLLECTION

"Mattie" got the next big kiss. She was Mrs. Martha Packer, of Boomer, a small town near the farm on which Pershing lived at one time. Then a withered old Negro crawled under the Pullman car and rose up right in front of the General.

"Hello, Al," was the greeting, then a big handshake and the General started to talk of days when Allen Warfield worked as "bus" driver for an old hotel in Laclede.

Looking around at the multitude General Pershing gave the same wide, happy smile to everyone. He radiated good spirit, making it hard to believe he had carried the reputation of being a man of iron discipline.

"There's lots of new ones grown up since I left here," and he patted children on the head, shook the hands of several manly-looking boys, and kissed a pretty little girl or two.

Eleven-year-old Warren Pershing got lost in the shuffle as the crowd slowly wiggled its way along the railroad track to intersect the main street of Laclede which leads to his home two blocks from the tracks.

Standing high above most of the crowd, General Pershing peered around and then called to a towheaded little rascal who was packed into the crowd, taking as little interest in the proceedings as though he were on the way to church.

Warren was given into the care of Clay Bigger, one of Pershing's closest friends, but broke away when reporters tried to get him to say something. Warren closed up like a clam, ducked his head, and took on an expression that matched exactly the pictures of his father in troop inspections.

When photographers and cinema men finally got a small space cleared to photograph General Pershing, Warren was nowhere to be seen. He was crouched down behind his father.

"Come on up here, Warren," the General pleaded. "I want your picture by my side here in my home town. It is a picture I'm going to prize."

Finally the Pershing home was reached, and when the General had mounted the steps there were cries for a speech. He smiled the well-known Pershing smile and shook his head. The calls for a speech became more insistent, however.

Finally he raised his right hand for silence and it was given

*without delay. The noise of bedlam changed instantly to a hush, with
no sound but the breathing of excited persons.*

*After a pause while he seemed to be collecting his thoughts to
put into words, he smiled and delivered his address. It was:*

"I'm mighty glad to be welcomed home by you, my friends."

The road back was a tough one, economically and socially. In the
first place, a very undemocratic omelet had to be unscrambled. Under
emergency legislation the government had taken over control of food
distribution and manufacture; also the coal supply and shipments, rail-
ways, telephone and telegraph were government run. And incidentally,
there were charges that some of the companies sabotaged their own
facilities, fearing permanent nationalization.

A voluntary labor-management armistice had been in operation, but
that blew up with a bang and there was an epidemic of crippling strikes
and other forms of labor unrest.

Washington had settled such labor relation problems as there had
been and completely controlled foreign commerce. Now the only worry
about foreign commerce was the lack of it.

A short puff of wartime prosperity collapsed. Prices sank. Unemploy-
ment rose until there were 5 million jobless. This contributed to frictions
and flare-ups, with the fiery crosses of the flourishing Ku Klux Klan
spreading racial and religious hatreds.

During 1920, Pershing spent much of his time in touring the Army
camps, where, even Chief of Staff March had to concede, the General
consistently appeared as "a magnificent figure of a man." Pershing's
first question to the commandant would be invariably, "Are the men getting everything they need?"

His increasing concern these days was for the security of the country
that he loved so deeply.

"Let's not delay longer," he told a meeting of officers of the 4th
Division at Camp Dodge, Iowa. "We must find the men who are leaders
of those who would overthrow the Government—and when we find them
let's convert or deport them, and do it immediately!"

On June 8, 1920, Pershing apparently wavered as to whether he
would be a candidate for the Republican Presidential nomination. In
Chicago, Major General Leonard Wood and Governor Frank Lowden,
of Illinois, were battling for the coveted title at their party's convention.

"I feel," he was quoted as saying, "that no patriotic American could

Pershing greets Captain Street, of the Alaska fliers group, at Bolling Field in October, 1920. The archenemy of the General of the Armies, retiring Chief of Staff, Major General Peyton C. March, is at the left. NATIONAL ARCHIVES

decline to serve in that high position if called upon to do so by the people."

He underscored the statement by requesting that he be placed upon the Army's retired list. That evening, in Highwood, his home on Rittenhouse Street in Washington's northwest section, he packed his suitcases.

The next morning, however, he received curt advice from Chicago: "Wait." The Republican party chieftains had other plans for breaking the Lowden-Wood deadlock.

On June 12, the nation heard the news: Warren G. Harding, an obscure senator from Ohio, had been nominated on the 10th ballot.

Pershing remained a military man.

The following year, he relieved Peyton March as Chief of Staff of the United States Army. The brief ceremony involving two near archenemies took place in the second-floor suite of the architecturally Victorian State, War and Navy Building, across from the White House.

It was July 1, 1921. There was no longer a Commander-in-Chief of the A.E.F. For that matter, there remained but a negligible remnant of the A.E.F., and that sampling all but absorbed by their German hosts.

As Chief of Staff Pershing blueprinted America's future armies, stressing a reorganization of the General Staff and establishing a positive training program of reserve components, including the Citizens Military Training Camps. U. S. ARMY PHOTOGRAPH

Ten days later, General of the Armies Pershing stood grim and erect on a Hoboken pier before the coffins of the first 7,264 war dead to be brought home.

"Only those who fought with them can ever know the height of religious devotion and patriotism to which they arose," declared their commander of 1917–18.

As Chief of Staff, Pershing did his best to keep alive past mistakes, and to counsel as to the future. He wrote, for example, in the *Saturday Evening Post:*

"Our plunge into the World War, in the face of all of our handicaps, was extremely courageous, but quite pathetic. One hesitates to contemplate the fate of Europe, and ourselves as well, if the grace of the Almighty, in His wise providence, had not seen fit to confuse our enemies and mercifully watch over our Allies for more than a year while we undertook to train 5,000,000 officers and men and to provide them with munitions, airplanes and transports. All we can say is that through the years we, the people, and those who make our laws, have gone from bad to worse, learning little, doing less, still prejudiced, lulled into inaction by an unwarranted sense of security and by false ideas of economy, instead of using plain, practical common sense and making reasonable provision in time of peace for the maintenance of a moderate policy of national defense.

"As individuals, with some important exceptions, our people are basically loyal and sound. Theirs is a most glorious and inspiring record of personal courage and devotion, striving in times of peril to overcome our deplorable want of national vision. In spite of the shackles of local political expedience, our wealth, resources and virility have carried us forward to the first rank among the powers of the world. Expanding international relations have become intimate and complicated, so that every individual must suffer or profit through their shifting status. Meanwhile the country has muddled through our wars, the people making heroic sacrifices on the battlefields and at home, and paying with monotonous regularity in blood and treasure the enormous penalty of ignoring nationally the plain and obvious lessons of history. The situation at home appears serious when we realize the extent to which the simple-minded have recently embraced impractical, unpatriotic and even destructive theories.

Flowers "from a friend" on the desk of the retiring Chief of Staff, September 13, 1924. PERSHING COLLECTION

A group of pacifists, who, by carrying placards and applying epithets, think they can end wars, proclaim in favor of our complete disarmament as a beginning to world peace, entirely ignoring the experience of the World War and the palpable fact that we should be in a class by ourselves and probably become at once the object of aggression by wiser nations. It is one of the inconsistencies of this group to be among the first to demand protection at home and intervention abroad."

But—nobody in America seemed to care any more: about anything. This was the jazz age, the speakeasy age, the flapper age. Harding himself had become at least the symbol of frivolity, corruption and dangerous national insularity.

A warmhearted man, however, he did manifest a certain solicitude toward the war veterans. He entertained wounded soldiers at frequent White House parties, and sent gifts of candy, cigarettes and flowers to the hospitals. But at the same time, he vetoed their bonus bill.

As one editorial bitterly observed, "The doughboys can't eat flowers."

What Pershing cried out in public did not fall on receptive national

Pershing had to limit greetings from little girls in public, after he broke down once in Memphis, when a curly-haired child handed him a bouquet of flowers, and found himself facing his audience with tears streaming down his cheeks. PERSHING COLLECTION

ears. So what if Germany had not really been beaten? Who wanted even a medium-sized standing army, or, for that matter, a modern one? The Navy was scuttled, scrapped, tied up at dozens of Navy yards to rust and become barnacled, otherwise relegated into third-rate impotency.

As Chief of Staff, there became little Pershing could do but blueprint the organization for a better U. S. Army of the future. And this he did, especially with respect to the General Staff, the National Guard, and Reserves.

On August 2, 1923, General Pershing, quite by coincidence, happened to be one of the last callers at the bedroom of President Harding in the Palace Hotel, San Francisco, before the Chief Executive's sudden passing. Pershing, visiting the Presidio which itself was rife with such tragic memories, was dining with his friend Colonel Stanton (who had said "Lafayette, we are here!") when the word of Harding's death was given him.

The Chief of Staff became a member of the funeral party which escorted the body of the dead President eastward. The train stopped at places large and small in response to surprising demonstrations of national grief, comparable even to the homage accorded Lincoln and McKinley.

After the burial, however, Pershing was tormented by considerable doubt as to whether his new President, Calvin Coolidge, from Vermont, would wish him to remain as Chief of Staff. For that matter, he had but a year remaining before he would be retired.

There came no word from the increasingly silent and noncommittal Executive Offices just across the street from his own offices. It was now mid-fall.

Finally, though he knew he should wait for a summons from his Commander-in-Chief, Pershing violated what seemed to him strict military protocol and requested an interview with Coolidge. The two men shook hands and then sat in penetrating silence for a minute or more.

"Mr. President," the General finally blurted in blushing embarrassment, "I must ask you a very important question."

And he proceeded to ask. Again there was a silence, finally broken by Coolidge clearing his throat and stating in his crisp New England accent:

"General, I'm surprised you should ask that question."

The interview was over. And Pershing still did not know the answer to the question that was haunting his days and nights.

Another week went by before the Chief of Staff finally implored a White House aide to intercede for him. Coolidge's reply ultimately was conveyed to the frustrated General: "Of course" the President meant for Pershing to remain on the job.

During a great part of the ensuing year Pershing was abroad, touring the battlefields, American cemeteries, and studying locations for memorials. He was in France, in February, 1924, when former President Wilson died.

He was home, by September, in time to retire, on his 64th birthday.

"As the clock strikes noon, Saturday," he stated flatly, "I retire. That's all there is to it."

"Black Jack" Pershing, however, had become a symbol, almost an American tradition. Nobody wanted to see him put on the shelf, even if few paid much attention to his disquieting prophecies. Newspapers were unanimous in their distress, the Cleveland *Plain Dealer*, for one, commenting:

> *No business firm would discharge a tried and efficient employee merely because he had passed his sixty-fifth birthday. But Army rules are rules, unelastic as the laws of the Medes and Persians; and when it comes to a matter of Congressional action there are enough votes swayed by the pacifist element and other special and pettily vindictive elements to prevent the doing of the sensible and gracious thing.*

Said the Baltimore *Sun*:

> *His retirement is a loss to the country; and there is no doubt that when the public becomes acquainted with the circumstances of his retirement, especially the sharp reduction in his pay, it will demand tardy justice for him. Pershing has never stooped to the more obvious devices to obtain popularity; and this very fact has strengthened his hold on the country.*

Pershing faced a pay cut of 50 per cent, which would reduce his income, even with allowances, to $10,125 a year.

"Everybody thanked him," wryly observed Will Rogers, "and nobody gave him anything. I guess they figure that at his age he only needs half a salary as he will only eat half as much and only need half as good a place to sleep."

The day before retirement, September 12, standing next to President Coolidge, he reviewed a Defense Day parade of 30,000 troops. It proved to a skeptical country that at least the standing army could muster that number, and—they could march.

That evening, at a farewell dinner, Pershing became the first Chief of Staff to speak over a coast-to-coast radio network.

"As I see it," he declared, "the defense of one's country is a religious as well as a patriotic duty. No man can be faithful to his religious obligations and fail in his duty to the nation.

"The system of defense that we stand for will become the surest guarantee of peace that could be devised."

At 11:30 A.M. Saturday, a huge basket of flowers, obliquely tagged *From a friend*, was placed upon General Pershing's broad mahogany desk. Major General John L. Hines, wartime commander of the 4th Division, his successor, stood modestly in the background as photographers exploded their trays of flash powder.

As the clock struck noon, John J. Pershing retired. And that was all there was to it.

The night before retirement, Pershing became the first Chief of Staff to address the nation by radio, on a coast-to-coast hookup. The boy from Missouri had seen a lot of scientific achievement since he went on the prowl for Indians in the '80's. NATIONAL ARCHIVES

13

With His Soldiers

PERSHING moved into a baroque old apartment at 2029 Connecticut Avenue. From his third-floor window he could see the Capitol, the Washington Monument, the State, War and Navy Building, much of the city. Half a block from his front door, another cavalryman—Major General George B. McClellan—was astride his horse in immobile bronze.

Yet this most recently retired Army officer of great distinction was far from ready for the rocking chair. In November, he packed up once again—for Chile. President Coolidge had designated him as a special ambassador to represent the United States in Peru during a historical celebration.

Pershing and his official party sailed on the battleship *Utah*. Before they came home in the spring they had toured, as good-will missionaries, most of the South American capitals, as well as those in Trinidad and Cuba. Coolidge was so well pleased with Pershing's receptions in Latin America that he immediately appointed him President of a plebiscite commission to give a judgment in the Tacna-Arica controversy between Chile and Peru.

An office down the hall from his former one as Chief of Staff, with the nameplate GENERAL OF THE ARMIES, was rarely tenanted except for an aide and a dozing Negro doorman. When he had completed his service on the Tacna-Arica plebiscite, he went to Europe as head of the American Battle Monuments Commission, a duty to which he applied

163

himself with the same tireless devotion as he had done as Commander-in-Chief of the A.E.F.

More than 30,000 war dead were left in France, in Belgium and in England. The least their nation could do was to make their final resting places ones of beauty and peace.

And so, by Pershing's direction, were created the Aisne-Marne, Meuse-Argonne, Oise-Aisne, St. Mihiel, Somme and Suresnes cemeteries in France; Flanders Field, in Belgium; and Brookwood, near London.

However, thought the General of the Armies, there must, as well, be monuments to remind future generations of the areas where these Americans fought and died: Cantigny and Montfaucon, Bellicourt and Audenarde, Kemmel, Belleau Wood, Blanc Mont, also at the port of Brest, and still others close by the cemeteries.

And so the retirement went for the General of the Armies. He traveled back and forth across the Atlantic, as familiar a figure in Paris and London as he was in Washington. He maintained a permanent office in the American Embassy, Paris.

He received honorary degrees from Oxford and Cambridge universities and from the University of St. Andrews in Scotland. He also was elected to the Académie des Sciences Morales et Politiques in Paris, a rare honor for a military man; and in America he was chosen a trustee of the National Geographic Society.

The son of Laclede, Missouri, had become cosmopolitan in identification, as well as in taste. It was not unusual to find him in the Louvre, the British Museum, or the Metropolitan Museum of Art in New York, a quiet, intent and always immaculately attired civilian.

By the same token, he was one of America's most sought-after elder citizens. He did not want for job offers or opportunities to lend his name to some project or product. Edwin E. Smith, of Pittsburgh, one of many who propositioned him in this latter respect, sought endorsement for his song:

> *General Pershing is his name, he*
> *Is the man that is known for*
> *Fame, God bless his loving, throbbing*
> *Heart—he tried to please you all.*

Other solicitations ranged from part interest in grain elevators in Buenos Aires to growing and merchandising coconuts in the Philippines and selling fire insurance in Chicago.

The General of the Armies did not "go on the shelf" after retirement, but became active head of the American Battle Monuments Commission. Here he is inspecting the ruins of a church at Montfaucon. AMERICAN BATTLE MONUMENTS COMMISSION

The Meuse-Argonne Cemetery at Romagne, considerably altered since 1919 when German prisoners worked on it. AMERICAN BATTLE MONUMENTS COMMISSION

The General of the Armies, however, had but one interest, and neither fame nor fortune was among its components. He had never forgotten "the boys" he had left in France. He could not do enough to care for their mortal remains or endeavor to keep alive their memory —and, still more important, their deeds.

"When the last bugle is sounded," he once observed, "I want to stand up with my soldiers."

His concern with the nation's future, nonetheless, continued in undiminished intensity. Into the 1930's, in speeches and in magazine articles, he kept appealing for leadership in the realms of politics, business, and scholarship, and for impeccable honesty in all levels of government.

"If the time ever comes when public offices can be virtually bought and sold, either directly or indirectly," he told the Kiwanis Club in Chicago, "then the downfall of the Republic will not be far off."

During this same time, Pershing was at work on his memoirs. Finally, holing up at White Sulphur Springs with a warrant officer, Charles B. Shaw, who had been a clerk at Chaumont, he tied his bulky and often diffuse research together. The result was *My Experiences in the World War,* in two volumes.

Factual, clear and occasionally garnished with hints of humor, the autobiography nonetheless did not risk a peek behind the elderly soldier's mask, which had become increasingly austere—and impenetrable. It did win him a Pulitzer prize.

Certainly not a man of letters in the scholastic sense, Pershing read, though not widely nor deeply. Among his friends he earned a reputation as a book borrower: books of the action and adventure category which found their most general appeal among teen-age boys.

The decade which was the 30's was perhaps the gloomiest in Pershing's life. Not only did he find himself writing condolences with increasing frequency to the widows of his classmates and other Army friends, but he was forced to watch, helpless from the sidelines, the approaching holocaust in Europe for the second time in less than half a century.

The supposedly better world that General Pershing had helped to create seemed ready to crumble again. All that was needed was a little push, a small spark, any otherwise inconsequential "incident."

With the dedication of the memorial on Romagne Heights of the Meuse-Argonne, his active work with the American Battle Monuments Commission was almost finished. He kept closer to Washington, living

For a few more years the old cavalryman indulged his favorite pastime. Here he is in 1928 in Bluemont, West Virginia, with his son. NATIONAL ARCHIVES (*Right*) In good, sunny weather, the retired general never missed a chance to watch a parade, right through the 1930's. PERSHING COLLECTION

now on the second floor of the Metropolitan Club, but a two-block walk from his offices in the State, War and Navy Building.

A gray, wrinkled man in his mid-70's, the General of the Armies nonetheless appeared occasionally at social functions, even brought pleasure to a few Washington hostesses by dancing with them. He was still adored by women. In return, he adored them.

Active, he nonetheless was not physically up to the life he had known through the war years. No longer did he ride horseback. In fact when his favorite mounts, Kidron and Jeff, died of old age, the General's predilection for that exercise seemed to expire with them.

When he walked, his pace was slower, more hesitant. At last, younger men could keep up with him. Surely there would never again be a duplication of his pajama-clad early-morning calisthenics at Chaumont.

When he picked up a good cigar now, he never lit it but meditatively chewed, and savored, it.

The General of the Armies had come to resemble, in visage and in habit, an illustrious predecessor, William Tecumseh Sherman, at the same age.

On May 13, 1937, Pershing was President Roosevelt's representative at the coronation of King George VI, of England. On August 1, he spoke at the dedication of the Montfaucon Memorial in the Argonne. It was a Doric shaft of granite, 175 feet high, surmounted by a figure, "Liberty."

"The last conflict," he asserted, "brought no profit to any one, but left many questions still unsettled. But they can not be settled by war. Yet the prospects for peace do not look promising. Hatred and suspicion still exist and armaments at enormous cost continue to grow. And if no cure is discovered for this temporary madness, we are in a hopeless state. . . ."

It was an eventful year for the 77-year-old Pershing. Home by winter, he was at the National Cathedral, in Washington, on December 7, at the consecration of the tomb and memorial to Lieutenant Norman T. Prince, killed in action in 1916, a year after he helped establish the Lafayette Escadrille.

"So long," he said, "as we continue to produce men like Norman Prince and those who come after him, just so long will our country and its cherished institutions remain. . . ."

At this time Hollywood, mindful of its aberrations in 1918, decided to do a serious motion picture of General Pershing, based on his own biography. Not averse to the idea, he expressed a preference for Gary Cooper as his impersonator.

In February, 1938, the tentative project was tabled indefinitely by the General's sudden illness. Stricken with a heart and kidney ailment in Tucson, Arizona, he lapsed into a coma. A special Army railroad car was draped in black and shunted to a siding near the hospital.

His death was confidently predicted to be but hours away.

Surviving classmates and close Army associates were asked to be ready to attend services in Arlington National Cemetery. There a plot was selected in the middle of the World War section where, according to his wishes, he would be ready on Judgment Day to "stand up with my soldiers."

Newsweek Magazine, certain that General Pershing would be dead by its next publication date, printed a color-cover portrait and an obituary-type review of his life.

It was almost as if Pershing had been made aware of these funeral preparations. Early one morning his doctor, Major General Shelley U. Marietta, tried one desperation antidote to jolt his patient back to consciousness. He led the General's long-time chauffeur, Sgt. S. C. Schaeffer, into the sickroom.

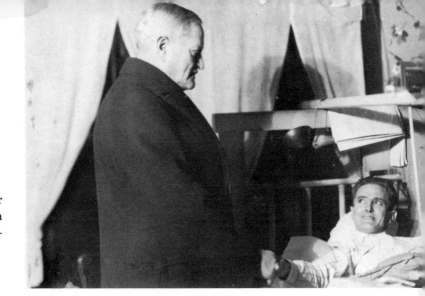

He never forgot his soldiers, or missed a chance to drop by a veterans hospital. PERSHING COLLECTION

A few months before Senator Warren's death, Pershing went walking with his distinguished father-in-law. PERSHING COLLECTION

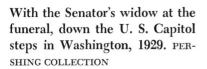

With the Senator's widow at the funeral, down the U. S. Capitol steps in Washington, 1929. PERSHING COLLECTION

"General," said the sergeant, leaning over the bed and whispering in fearful apprehension, "do you know who this is?"

To the profound surprise of Dr. Marietta, the nurses, and particularly, the chauffeur, Pershing opened his eyes for the first time in several days and snapped, "I don't know what you call yourself now, but you used to be Sgt. Schaeffer!"

His recovery was miraculously swift from that moment on. It was as though "Black Jack" were subconsciously attempting to prove the latent truth of the old saying: "The only way to get rid of a Cavalry officer is to shoot him!"

The black crepe and the black muslin were hurriedly ripped off the railway car and in a few days Pershing, chewing on a cigar, was riding in it—back to Washington. At the Union Station, leaning slightly on a cane but supported by none of his attendants, he stepped onto the platform and aimed a scowl at the semicircle of reporters and photographers awaiting him.

Lurking far back now in that scowl, which the fourth estate had grown accustomed to receive, was a certain triumphant gleam.

He took up residence in Walter Reed Hospital. His health returned, and soon he could be seen walking about the hospital grounds or being driven through Rock Creek Park. Increasingly testy, however, he was developing an obsession against being photographed, even when the Chief of the Signal Corps broached the matter as a personal favor.

"To hell with the War Department!" he once growled, waving his cane. "They can't make me have my picture taken!"

Possibly, his aversion found its roots in his grayish-white hair, wrinkled and otherwise withered appearance. Surely he was not the robust, smiling General Pershing who, even as recently as 1919, had smartly led the victory parade down Pennsylvania Avenue.

However, he wrote to his old friend Bernard M. Baruch, who had headed the War Industries Board, that he was feeling all right.

"Dear Bernie," he commenced, "in most respects I am in very good shape again. It is only my old trouble with rheumatism or arthritis or whatever it may be in the legs that is holding me down. I get out for an automobile ride nearly every day and am doing some walking, but this restricted life gets mighty irksome. I think it will end soon. . . . I am hoping to go abroad soon."

True to his word, Pershing went overseas—arriving in France on

May 31, 1939. He was back at the battlefields, once again paying his respects to his soldiers.

Returning August 17, aboard the U. S. Liner *Manhattan*, he told reporters that the French army seemed "ready," and he adjudged it in "excellent shape." Perhaps the General of the Armies spoke out of loyalty, past camaraderie.

At the same time, he warned that regular and reserve armed forces in the United States were far from adequate. As to the possible course of the future, Pershing was too canny to predict.

The world, as the editorial writers sized it up, was rushing hell-bent toward Armageddon. And on September 1, it happened. Hitler sent his well-readied military hordes crashing into Poland.

"The Polish state has rejected my efforts to establish neighborly relations and instead has appealed to weapons," was Chancellor Hitler's ranting manifesto. "To put an end to these insane incitations nothing remains but for me to meet force with force from now on. The German army will conduct and fight for honor and the right to the life of the resurrected German people with firm determination. I expect that every soldier, mindful of the great traditions of the eternal German military, will do his duty to the last. . . . Long live our people and our Reich!"

World War II had come.

On October 31, Pershing, from his fourth-floor suite in a wing of Walter Reed especially constructed for his use, wrote once more to "Bernie" Baruch.

"The war abroad," he penned, "seems to have taken a rather unique turn. I had expected considerable more activity on both sides than has taken place and am now under the impression that effort is being made to bring about some understanding that will prevent the frightful loss of life that modern war involves. I know nothing about what is being done, of course, but the fact that nobody wants war would seem to me to be sufficient grounds for hoping that something may come out of it besides disastrous destruction."

Hoping, as it turned out, was not enough. Soon, America was embroiled once more in a foreign conflict. Putting on a neat, blue-serge suit, General Pershing, cane in hand, assisted by only one aide, left for the White House. There he offered his "services" to his country.

"General Pershing," President Roosevelt said with heartfelt admiration, "you are magnificent."

Certain of his "boys" of World War I, including the now generals Marshall, Patton and MacArthur, became his favorites of the new conflict. A word conveyed to them from the old Commander-in-Chief of the A.E.F. bore significant weight in the selection of other officers.

As to General Marshall, he had urged President Roosevelt to keep him home, where, the aged soldier reasoned, some of the most important work of this war was to be effected.

In 1942, he commented on the nation's newest breed of fightingman in a letter to the Class of '86:

"I am sure that all of you have thrilled as I have, to the heroic defense that our soldiers have made on Bataan. There are and have been no better fighters in the world than the American soldiers, and given anything like an even chance they can be depended upon to do more than hold their own. On the home front, it seems to me that we have not profited as we should have done from the lessons of the World War, but we do seem to be hitting our stride at last. It is disappointing to be forced to sit on the sidelines in stirring times like these, but we of '86 have had our day and must realize the limitations of our years."

In his Walter Reed suite he received such personages as Churchill, Field Marshal Montgomery and General de Gaulle. He embarrassed the latter by inquiring as to the health of "my old friend Pétain." The onetime hero of Verdun was in disgrace through his heading of the Vichy government, held to be traitorous by most Frenchmen.

Now Pershing could politely say, "I told you so," without fear of contradiction.

"If we had gone to Berlin then," he asserted in 1944, "we would not be going there now."

The General of the Armies maintained an avid interest in the war's progress, insisting on seeing copies of the current battle maps. At one time, he expressed a desire to be flown overseas and observe the vast conflict at first hand.

Exceptionally alert considering his age and able to adjust his concepts of warfare, he was fascinated by the use of airpower. After all, he himself had made extensive use of it in World War I's last great battle: the Argonne. By the end of October, 1918, multiple groups of 200 or more planes each were not uncommon sights above the trenches.

Pershing, too, was both intrigued and appalled by the A-bomb in an understandable complex of emotion. After the war, he requested and was given secret reports on the Bikini tests.

All in all, he maintained health and acuity. No longer able to leave his suite, he nonetheless ate well, enjoying such staples as bean soup and steak. He was read to by the hour, nurses and Gray Ladies alternating with his devoted sister, Miss May Pershing.

On October 17, 1947, Pershing received a special medal authorized by Congress, "in recognition of his peerless leadership, heroic achievements and great military victories as Commander-in-Chief of the American Expeditionary Forces in Europe in World War I, and for his gallant and unselfish devotion to the service of his country in his contribution to the preparation for and the prosecution of World War II."

His son, daughter-in-law, and sister were present. So were Brigadier General T. Bentley Mott (retired), a West Point classmate, and Lieutenant Colonel Ralph Curtin, a wartime aide. There were, however, few remaining of his old friends.

It seemed not improbable that the General of the Armies would make at least his 90th year, and then start on that long, lonely road to the century mark.

In 1944, the aging General of the Armies was visited at his suite in Walter Reed Hospital by General De Gaulle. Pershing kept up an active interest in the prosecution of the war and in modern armament. U. S. ARMY PHOTOGRAPH

Old soldiers, however, fade away. . . .
U. S. ARMY PHOTOGRAPH

Yet the old gentleman was growing weaker. He had suffered at least one stroke, and was enfeebled by the common nemesis of burdensome years: arteriosclerosis. Once, when an Army band serenaded him from the sunken gardens below his suite, his sister and a nurse helped him to the window to acknowledge the musical greeting.

Bent, weak and ashen-faced, he presented a pathetic and altogether disquieting figure.

There was little left for the General of the Armies by 1948 except his memories: of places like Laclede and Fort Bayard, Pine Ridge, the University of Nebraska, Mindanao, Fort Bliss, and the astral profusion of French geographical entities whose names he never could spell. There were battles and patrols and, simply, periods of command duty for the old General to reflect upon that extended back to Indian fighting days.

He had outlived Bliss and Liggett and Bullard, Summerall, Dickman and Menoher, Harbord, Hines and Omar Bundy—almost all of his wartime generals, and nearly all of his West Point classmates. Avery Andrews and Peyton March were among the signal, resilient exceptions.

. . . General Pershing possessed memories both happy and bitter, of a good life, an active life, a dedicated life and, at times, a blindly

. . . and they do die. In Arlington National Cemetery, beneath an enlisted man's marker, Pershing was given every opportunity to realize, in another life, his last wish:

"When the last bugle is sounded, I want to stand up with my soldiers." U. S. ARMY PHOTOGRAPH

cruel one. Certainly at the Presidio that August night, 1915, a great deal more had died than his wife and three daughters.

The loss had altered the entire course of Brigadier General Pershing's life—steeled him, annealed his emotions and, to a certain extent, woven iron mesh about his compassion. He had become a driven man, a man who finds solace only in a personal kind of sublimation, and even headlong flight. But in so doing he had immeasurably aided in the winning of a war.

Time, however, was at long last running out. If, in some respects, it was sentence he was serving, pardon was nearing. Now, it was almost as though what John Pershing had done, where he had been, whom he had known and what he had believed were but dreams, figments out of another world. The old man was slipping away, and in this mystifying, continuing cycle of human creation—and destruction—it all seemed entirely preposterous.

At 3:50 A.M., on a mild July night, General Marietta, summoned by a suddenly apprehensive night nurse, put his stethoscope to his patient's chest. He moved the instrument around to other positions, listened intently, then straightened up again.

He walked into an adjoining room and called Miss May Pershing and Warren Pershing.

. . . A summer day would be dawning, a day with all its wonder and enigma which the world would pursue for the first time in nearly 88 years without being able to count John Joseph Pershing among its living.

It was a Thursday, July 15, 1948.

Another day was about to lighten the horizon, a day which would find the world sorely troubled. In Berlin, an airlift was attempting to thwart the Russian blockade. Jews and Arabs were fighting to the death in Palestine. The Balkans were aflame with Communism.

In China and Russia the hand of the despot was terrible, and certain. Countries such as Lithuania, Estonia and Latvia had vanished completely from the maps.

The world—even as on a long-ago morning, September 13, 1860—was unhappy, distraught. Hate, fear, and unconscionable inhumanity were scourging the face of the earth.

General Pershing had striven to the utmost of his ability to make it a better world, and it was everyone's tragedy that his efforts had been so ill rewarded.

He deserved a far, far better requiem.

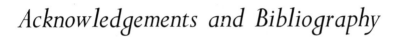

Acknowledgements and Bibliography

Acknowledgments

The Editors of the Army Times Publishing Company are indebted to many people, many organizations, many libraries, many companies, many newspapers, magazines and other publications (both past and present) without whose aid this biography of the General of the Armies would not have been possible.

So many individuals gave unstintingly in time and suggestions—whether of a historical, briefly anecdotal or of a source lead nature—that the task of listing all without unintentionally omitting some becomes impractical, if not virtually impossible.

From the text, however, it may be fairly assumed that contemporaries such as Warren Pershing, General Shelley Marietta and Colonel Charles B. Shaw were of especial assistance.

As indicated in the Foreword, the basic material for this study originated in the Manuscript Division of the Library of Congress where —for some not readily apparent reason—the vast Pershing Papers collection has reposed untouched for eight years. Included, for example, is the unpublished manuscript of his memoirs chronicling his life until his war years.

Photographs reproduced in this book originated primarily in this collection, from the Prints and Photographs Division of the Library of Congress, from the National Archives, the Signal Corps, the American Battle Monuments Commission, and Walter Reed Hospital.

Appreciation is also expressed to the Magazine and Book Branch, Department of the Army; the U.S. Military Academy, West Point; First Army Headquarters, Governors Island; the New York Public Library; and the District of Columbia Public Library.

Especially illuminating on the General's early years were the articles written during and immediately after the war period by George Mac-

Adam in *The World's Work*. Other magazines consulted in the course of research include:

American Magazine
The Army and Navy Register
Atlantic
Collier's
Current History
The Forum
Hesperian
(student publication, University
  of Nebraska)

Illustrated London News
Literary Digest
London *Graphic*
The National Geographic
Outlook
Punch
Saturday Evening Post

These newspapers proved of value:

Atlanta *Journal*
Baltimore *Sun*
Boston *Globe*
Chicago *Tribune*
Christian Science Monitor
Kansas City *Star*
New York *Herald*
The New York Times
(including its publication of the
  war years: *Current History*)

Philadelphia *Inquirer*
Pittsburgh *Post*
Richmond *News Leader*
St. Louis *Post Dispatch*
St. Louis *Globe Democrat*
(Washington) *Evening Star*
Washington *Post*

The files of the original Army publication, *The Stars and Stripes,* also were rich in source material.

In addition, special mention should be made of that historian's delight, *The London Times*, with a comprehensive index extending back to within a few years of the American Revolution.

The Associated Press, United Press, International News Service and Reuter's furnished, as usual, authentic wire service background news for the biography.

Special credit is due the Putnam's editors, Howard Cady and Lois Dwight Cole, not only for their vision but their patience as well.

Among those of the Army Times Publishing Co. who assisted in the production were H. R. Baukhage, Col. Stephen Tillman, Col. John Virden and—last but by no means least—the company publisher, president and editorial adviser-confessor, Melvin E. Ryder.

A. A. HOEHLING, *Project Editor*

Bibliography

Andrews, Avery, *My Friend and Classmate John J. Pershing*. Military Service Publishing Co., Harrisburg, 1939

Benwell, Harry A., *History of the Yankee Division*. The Cornhill Co., Boston, 1919

Baker, Newton D., *Why We Went to War*. Harper and Brothers, New York, 1936

Broun, Heywood, *The A.E.F.* D. Appleton, New York, 1918

Bullard, Robert Lee, *Personalities and Reminiscences of the War*. Doubleday Page, New York, 1925

Crowell, Benedict, *How America Went to War*. Yale University Press, New Haven, 1921

Damrosch, Walter, *My Musical Life*. Charles Scribner's Sons, New York, 1937

Daniels, Josephus, *The Wilson Era*. University of North Carolina Press, Chapel Hill, 1946

Davis, Richard Harding, *The Cuban and Porto Rican Campaigns*. Charles Scribner's Sons, New York, 1898

Dawes, Charles G., *A Journal of The Great War*. Houghton Mifflin, Boston, 1921

Forrest, Wilbur, *Behind the Front Page*. D. Appleton-Century, New York, 1934

Gibbons, Floyd, *And They Thought We Wouldn't Fight*. George H. Doran, New York, 1918

Harbord, James G., *The American Army in France*. Little Brown, Boston, 1936

Hendricks, Burton J., *The Life and Letters of Walter Hines Page*. Garden City Publishing Co., New York, 1927

Hindenburg, Marshal Paul von, *Out of My Life*. Cassell, London, 1920

Janis, Elsie, *So Far So Good*. E. P. Dutton, New York, 1932

Judy, Capt. Will, *A Soldier's Diary*. Judy Publishing Co., Chicago, 1930

Lansing, Robert, *War Memoirs*. Bobbs Merrill, Indianapolis, 1935

Lejeune, John A., *The Reminiscences of a Marine*. Dorrance and Co., Philadelphia, 1930

March, Francis A., *History of the World War*. United Publishers, Philadelphia, 1919

March, Peyton, *The Nation at War*. Doubleday Doran and Co., New York, 1932

Michelin (Guide), *The Americans in the Great War*. Paris, 1920

Palmer, Maj. Frederick, *America in France*. Dodd Mead, New York, 1918

Palmer, Frederick, *John J. Pershing*. Military Service Publishing Co., Harrisburg, 1939

Pershing, John J., *Final Report of Gen. John J. Pershing, Commander-in-Chief American Expeditionary Forces*. Government Printing Office, Washington, 1919

Pershing, John J., *My Experiences in the World War*. Frederick A. Stokes, New York, 1931

Russell, Henry, *The First Division*. Crescent Press, Pittsburgh, 1920

Seeger, Alan, *Poems*. Charles Scribner's Sons, New York, 1916

Simonds, Frank H., *History of the World War*. Doubleday Page, New York, 1918

Sullivan, Mark, *Our Times*. Charles Scribner's Sons, New York, 1936

Tompkins, Col. Frank, *Chasing Villa*. The Military Service Publishing Co., Harrisburg, 1934

White, William Allen, *The Martial Adventures of Henry and Me*. Macmillan, New York, 1918.

Cyclone
38th Division

Blue and Gray
29th Division

The Red One
1st Division

Blue Ridge
80th Division

Golden Arrow
8th Division

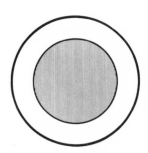

Buckeye
37th Division

Keystone
28th Division

Hourglass
7th Division

Wildcat
81st Division

DATE DUE